CREATING PEACE BY
BEING PEACE

CREATING PEACE BY BEING PEACE

The Essene Sevenfold Path

REBBE GABRIEL COUSENS, MD

Foreword by JOHN ROBBINS

North Atlantic Books
Berkeley, California

Published by
North Atlantic Books
P.O. Box 12327
Berkeley, California 94712

Cover and book design by Suzanne Albertson
Printed in the United States of America

Creating Peace by Being Peace: The Essene Sevenfold Path is sponsored by the Society for the Study of Native Arts and Sciences, a nonprofit educational corporation whose goals are to develop an educational and cross-cultural perspective linking various scientific, social, and artistic fields; to nurture a holistic view of arts, sciences, humanities, and healing; and to publish and distribute literature on the relationship of mind, body, and nature.

North Atlantic Books' publications are available through most bookstores. For further information, call 800-733-3000 or visit our website at www.northatlanticbooks.com.

Library of Congress Cataloging-in-Publication Data

Cousens, Gabriel, 1943–
    Creating peace by being peace : the Essene sevenfold path / Gabriel Cousens ; foreword by John Robbins.
        p. cm.
    Summary: "Focuses on bringing peace to the world and integrates the ancient wisdom of the Essenes with a new awareness of the urgent need for humankind to undergo a spiritual awakening"—Provided by publisher.
    Includes bibliographical references and index.
        ISBN 978-1-55643-722-9
    1. Peace—Religious aspects. 2. Essenes. 3. New Age movement. I. Title.
    BL65.P4C68 2008
    299'.93—dc22   2008005201

2 3 4 5 6 7 8 9 UNITED   14 13 12 11 10 09

Dedication

TO DR. EDMOND BORDEAUX SZEKELY, whose genius and Renaissance awareness have made volumes of translated books about the Essenes available to the world. Dr. Szekely was a true luminary who inspired the author with his clarity and depth of understanding of the Essene Way of Life and the Sevenfold Path of Peace.

To Swami Muktananda Paramahansa, the author's first enlightened spiritual teacher, without whose transmission of grace and guidance in this one's spiritual unfoldment this book could not have been written.

To Swami Prakashananda Saraswati, this one's second enlightened spiritual teacher, whose personal guidance and "Agaram Bagaram" life have been a source of continual inspiration, love, and spiritually sophisticated understanding of Gabriel's post-enlightenment maturing.

To Shanti, Gabriel's soulmate and life partner, who actively lives and shares the truth of the Sevenfold Path of Peace with her beloved and is a constant source of inspiration.

To Gabriel's wonderful children, Rafael and Heather, and grandchildren, Rhea and Katja. May you know peace in your generations.

To all the grandfathers and grandmothers and other noble souls inspired to transition into the Culture of Life and Liberation for themselves and the sake of succeeding generations.

And to the teachings of the Torah and of the prophets who have come before us and have shared the following teachings.

An ancient tradition says that each of the six hundred thousand people present at the communication of the Torah (the ever-renewing teaching given to Moses by God on Mount Sinai, without punctuation, and with at least four levels of interpretation so that it may be reinterpreted anew in each generation, also known as the Old Testament) were given at least one section to interpret and share as a teaching with their brothers and sisters. In each generation these meaningful teachings of ancient wisdom are passed forward. In this book Gabriel shares several teachings related to peace.

> I will put my Torah in their inner parts, and write it in their hearts; and will be their God, and they shall be my people; and they shall teach no more every man his neighbor, and every man his brother, saying, "Know the Lord"; for they shall all know Me, from the least of them to the greatest of them, sayeth the Lord.
>
> Jeremiah 31:32

The Torah is the living cosmic Truth of the Nothing *(Ein Sof)* that is already encoded in our "inner parts" (our spiritual anatomy) and heart. The Culture of Life and Liberation is presently activating these holographic patterns, which are essential for creating world peace as the result of the activation of ourselves as a living prayer of peace.

> Get thee out of thy country, and from thy kindred, and from thy father's house, unto the land that I will show thee.
>
> Genesis 12:1

God as the name El Shaddai (the nurturer) instructs Avraham, "Lech Lecha." From the viewpoint of the Culture of Life and Liberation and the Sevenfold Path of Peace, this means "Go to the Self" (I Am That). To do this one must let go of attachments and ego identifications with parents, culture, country, thought forms, illusion of the personality, and all identification with the body-mind-I Am complex; let go and surrender into the Divine Self. This book is a blessing to inspire and support the reader in the eternal journey of Lech Lecha. In the Divine Presence of the inner self, emanating out of the silence of the Self is the direct knowledge of Peace, the Pearl of Great Price, and the most cherished awareness an Essene may hold.

And the wolf shall dwell with the lamb, and the leopard shall lie down with the kid; and the calf and the young lion and the fatling together; and a little child shall lead them. And the cow and the bear shall feed; their young ones shall lie down together: and the lion shall eat straw like the ox. And the suckling child play on the hole of the cobra, and the weaned child shall put his hand on the viper's nest. They shall not hurt or destroy in all my holy mountain: for the earth shall be full of the knowledge of the Lord.

Isaiah 11:6–10

And God said, Behold I have given you every herb bearing seed, which is upon the face of all the earth, and every tree, on which is the fruit yielding seed: to you it shall be for food. And to every beast of the earth and to every bird of the air, and to every thing that creeps on the earth, wherein there is life, I have given every green herb for food: and it was so.

Genesis 1:29

These two quoted passages speak to a deep meaning of world peace. The holographic expression of peace will be so strong in every species that even the carnivorous animals, including humans, will return to a plant-source-only diet again and return to the teachings of Genesis 1:29. Genesis 1:29 describes the original biblical diet, which not only brings peace to the body and has the potential to prevent or heal most chronic diseases such as diabetes, but helps us return to the Culture of Life and Liberation from the planetary and personal misery caused by a Culture of Death lifestyle. Although we cannot eat our way to God, this biblical cuisine creates a normal brain chemistry and awakens consciousness.

And He shall judge between many peoples, and shall decide concerning mighty nations afar off; and they shall beat their swords into plowshares, and their spears into pruning hooks; nation shall not lift up sword against nation, neither shall they learn war any more.

Micah 4:3 and Isaiah 2:4

In the flaming power of the Divine Presence, the ego, which is the source of all war, is burned up. The egoic domination of consciousness, which is the source of power of the Culture of Death, is incinerated into ashes, and out of these ashes arises the Culture of Life and Liberation, in which consciousness guides the ego into proper service to the unspoken will of God.

You shall love your neighbor as yourself.

Leviticus 19:18

As the great Rabbi Hillel taught in the first century BCE, this is the essence of the Torah. This was later affirmed as a major Torah principle by Rabbi Akiba in the second century AD. The only problem is that most people's self-esteem is so low that they hate their neighbor as themselves and their ego often seeks revenge or honor killings in order to at least temporarily boost their self-esteem. So this is meant to be understood as "Love your neighbor as your Divine Self." When you are in touch with your Divine Self you see the same Self, or spark of God, in all people. This is the Essene awareness of *hishtavut* (seeing God in all of creation equally). It is from this perspective that "They shall not hurt or destroy in all of my holy mountain."

It is from the spiritual power of the awareness of the One that peace will emerge as the predominant consciousness on the planet. In the awareness of the Divine Presence there is only peace on all seven levels.

The final dedication is to the Divine, the source of all.

Rebbe Gabriel Cousens, MD

Acknowledgments

THE AUTHOR WOULD LIKE TO EXPRESS HIS LOVE and gratitude to Shanti Golds Cousens, who, through her love and our marriage, has helped further integrate the living of creating peace by being peace into the author's life in a heartfelt way. The author thanks Rafael and Heather Cousens, his two wonderful children, who now have children of their own, for sharing their love and support and for their unique contribution to the author's life.

The author thanks the reader for understanding the point the author makes by speaking in the third person—that we are not the body-mind-I Am complex, but that which is prior to those three-dimensional concepts of the 1-percent reality, the 99-percent reality of the living biophoton field as the spark of the Divine as part of the flaming living field of the One.

The author also thanks his supporting staff at the Tree of Life, especially Michael Bedar and Santi Krause, who helped edit and format the book as well as update the peace resources. He also thanks Michael Ratner for the introduction, time spent proofing and editing the manuscript, and involving Steve Robertson as the major contributor to the music section; Fabian Alsultany, director of GlobeSonic Entertainment (GlobeSonic.com) for his insight into cultural peace through music; and Jessica Bennet for the extended time spent making insightful suggestions about the content and form of the book.

The author wants to thank John Robbins for the poetic wisdom of his Foreword, as well as his friends in the service of peace: Rev. Michael Beckwith, Rabbi Michael Lerner, James Twyman, and Rabbi Lynn Gottlieb. The author extends thanks also to J. J. and Desiree Hurtak, who have worked ceaselessly for peace. Thanks are extended to Gregg Braden, who has contributed significant theoretical work in his books exploring the biophysics of peace meditations and the power of living prayer. All of these great souls have inspired Gabriel with their dedication to creating world peace, and he is most grateful.

The author is most grateful for the support and encouragement of North Atlantic Books and the author's visionary publisher, Richard Grossinger, for standing behind books such as this, and for the editorial staff lead by Emily Boyd.

The author expresses gratitude to his spiritual brothers and sisters in different traditions who have come together in peace meditations and ceremonies, and who are living the creating peace by being peace consciousness. The author is grateful for those who are part of the yearly Spirit Dances at the Tree of Life in Patagonia, Arizona, and the Tree of Light Foundation in Israel; to the staff at the Tree of Life in the United States who have chosen to lead their lives as beacons of light and love for the world; to the public who reads this book and chooses to open the heart to the message; and to those who have chosen to become the living prayer that is transforming this world, slowly but surely, into a world resonating with the vibrations of peace, love, and compassion.

Contents

Foreword

SOMETHING IS SHIFTING IN OUR TIME. As the future of life on earth is seen to be fundamentally in jeopardy, a wave of new awareness is sweeping across the planet. Everywhere people are seeing that if we continue to experience ourselves as isolated and threatened, if we continue to act as though our lives depended on conquering nature and each other, we will destroy not only ourselves but the very life-support systems that have given us birth. Everywhere there are people who are sensing the transformation that is called for if we are to continue. Everywhere there are people awakening to the possibility that life can have meaning, purpose, and pleasure when lived in accord with our deepest instincts for survival.

A spiritual instinct is arising in the collective human psyche. It is calling us out of our personal black holes, out of our hiding places and unconsciousness, and drawing us to life.

The truths of our time necessitate great changes in our ways of thinking and living. The old paradigms are giving way to ones more in keeping with the new potential to which our lives must now give expression.

As we move together into the uncharted realms of the future, few things are more important than drawing guidance from the deepest wisdom teachings of our past. For there has always lain in the human psyche the awareness of Universal Truths, and guidance to the steps involved in the so-very-human effort to bring our lives into alignment.

Creating Peace by Being Peace: The Essene Sevenfold Path by Rebbe Gabriel Cousens, MD, is at once a guide to the steps we are asked to take, and at the same time a call to deep layers of remembrance in our beings. We are shown the way to rejoin in harmony with the rest of Creation, and to open our lives to the blessings of the Great Spirit.

It is an ancient wisdom that is drawing us into the new. *Creating Peace by Being Peace: The Essene Sevenfold Path* helps us hear the way it speaks to us personally, individually. It is a call to make our lifestyles spiritual statements. It is a call to survival. Today, these have become the same task.

John Robbins
Founder and Chairman Emeritus of Board of Directors of EarthSave International
Author of *Diet for a New America, The Food Revolution,* and *Healthy at 100*
www.earthsave.org
www.foodrevolution.org

Introductions to the Author

Nothing can bring peace but yourself.

                                              Ralph Waldo Emerson

*If we want to save the world, we must have a plan. But no plan
will work unless we meditate.*

                                          His Holiness the Dalai Lama

*Since wars began in the minds of men, it is in the minds of
men that the defense of peace must be constructed.*

                                          UNESCO constitutional principle

IT WAS ON THE MILLENNIAL NEW YEAR'S EVE when I first got to meet Gabriel
Cousens, MD, face to face at his Tree of Life eco-spiritual healing center
in Patagonia, Arizona, as we were about to participate in an American
Native Sweat Lodge ceremony to welcome in the new century. Dr. Cousens
was busy that weekend accommodating esteemed guests and visitors while
leading the ceremony. That cold December weekend Gabriel also dedicated a peace pole connecting Patagonia to many other sister cities that
were engaged in the same activity. Thus began my relationship with Gabriel
and his work.

The same year I met Gabriel in person the United Nations General
Assembly proclaimed 2000 as the International Year for the Culture of
Peace. Although Gabriel had been living peace and teaching his conscious
awakening to "I Am That" for well over thirty years, it happened there on
that chilly New Year's eventful evening I first heard the term "Culture of
Life and Liberation."

In this book, Gabriel refers to himself in the third person as "the author"
or "Gabriel" to make a clear teaching. It is a message that Gabriel is communicating—in essence, that the body-mind complex isn't who he is

identified with and as a teaching to all that the personality is a case of mistaken identity. The I Am is identified with consciousness, not the body-mind complex also known as the ego, which we also know as the personality. So, he uses the third person as a basic reminder of what the truth is. It helps the reader understand it in that context. Don't let it confuse you. It is an aid as a way of not identifying with who is talking, but with the consciousness behind the personality.

My point in highlighting this is that Gabriel teaches that if the whole world were no longer identified with personal form and thought forms, which are extensions of the ego, there would be no war.

My curiosity about what was implied led to many meetings with Gabriel: attending his public talks, media interviews, and eventually a weekly Internet radio program hosted by Gabriel. I feel fortunate in our strong bond that has continued to grow, partnering in the endeavor to bring peace to all. In the eight years passing, I have had the fortune of witnessing firsthand the successful evolution of his work and profound impact that can be found worldwide, starting from both American continents to Europe, Australia, India, Egypt, Morocco, Hong Kong, Lebanon, and Israel to wherever Gabriel travels. People from many divergent places have found his insights helpful and indigenous cultures across the globe have adopted his conscious eating, vegan "living food" diet and spiritual nutrition practices remarkable in reversing chronic degenerative diseases such as diabetes, and generally improving health, spiritual awareness, world peace, and even flexibility for yoga. Millions worldwide have read his books. I have met many who have trekked thousands of miles just to meet Rebbe Gabriel Cousens, MD, to see a talk in person, to gain a firsthand knowledge of his six foundations for supporting spiritual life and inner peace, and to receive Shaktipat.

Gabriel's deep personal experience in the Jewish, Essene, kabbalistic, Native American, and Yogic traditions have allowed him to penetrate to the essence of spiritual life in the different traditions in a way that transcends the ego and ethnocentric perceptions that have become such a source of conflict and confusion in the world. This background enhances his ability to provide humanitarian services in a variety of culturally diverse situations. Currently, the focus of Gabriel's humanitarian work is creating world peace on all levels. He has been leading peace meditations around the world since 1985. He established Peace 21, a meditation for peace four times per year on each equinox and solstice. In 1996, he established this quarterly peace meditation at the United Nations in New York. This is all part of an overall process to create peace and healing of the planet on the physical, mental, and spiritual levels. In 2003 he initiated the worldwide Peace Every Day Initiative™ to encourage all traditions to work for peace. This peace initiative has the endorsement of such diverse spiritual leaders as Rabbi Zalman Schachter-Shalomi, the grandfather of the Jewish Renewal Movement, Reverend Michael Beckwith, and Ahmed Costas, head of Islamic affairs of the Kingdom of Morocco. The Dalai Lama has also given his blessing to the project.

It is the purpose in rewriting the Sevenfold Path of Peace book to reach a new generation of readers and peace providers whose goal in life is not only achieve peace within themselves but to help forge the creation of a Culture of Life and Liberation that will give access to this ancient teaching so thoroughly needed in this present time.

Having personally worked with celebrities, motivational speakers, and prominent world leaders, Rebbe Gabriel Cousens, MD, is refreshingly unique because his wisdom is above the fray. Gabriel works daily on an individual level with people who are seeking to consciously cultivate peace in their own lives and in their families and communities. That is why I highly recommend reading this book and sharing these Essene insights by gifting multiple copies to your family and community.

May the Blessings Be,

Michael D. Ratner

Founder of the Friendship Fellowship and the Community Conversations Project

www.PeaceConference.org

There have been a few times in my life when I heard great things about a person before meeting him or her, then hoped that the reputation matched the real person. Gabriel Cousens is one of those people, and I'm happy to say that I was far from disappointed. He is a man whose dedication to peace extends far beyond his words. He lives what he believes, which can be a rare thing in this world. He is a man of high spiritual integrity, and I'm honored to support his vision of peace.

James Twyman
Author of *The Art of Spiritual Peacemaking, Emissary of Light,* and *The Moses Code* and director of the movie *The Moses Code*

Creating Peace by Being Peace is Rebbe Gabriel Cousens's compassionate vision of life. Rebbe Gabriel transmits ancient and universal teachings that the way of peace is an integrated and holistic approach to living that begins with our own bodies and moves in concentric circles to our families, community, cultural neighbors, and Mother Earth. Drawing upon his understanding of Jewish mysticism, yoga, Native American teachings, the wisdom of sages throughout time, and his vision of Essene teachings, Rebbe Gabriel offers the reader a comprehensive and practical vision of what he calls the Culture of Life and Liberation.

In a time when many people recognize the threat humans are imposing upon the life of the planet by war and environmental degradation, Rebbe Gabriel provides readers with an inspiring pathway of vegan diet, meditation, prayer, peacemaking consciousness, and devotional service. Peace begins with our daily choices to simplify our living, embrace forgiveness, and focus our awareness on the interconnectedness of all beings. In our search for guidance, seekers of peace and nonviolence can drink in the wisdom of a person dedicated to healing the human spirit in ways that are accessible and nurturing.

I deeply enjoyed reading *Creating Peace by Being Peace.* Each one of us can contribute to the creation of new consciousness on earth that will transform hearts and turn us away from destruction. Rebbe Gabriel's work can guide us along the way.

Rabbi Lynn Gottlieb
Co-founder of Shomer Shalom Institute for Jewish Nonviolence

Author's Introduction

WE CAN ACTUALLY CHOOSE TO CREATE PEACE BY BEING PEACE. One who is at peace brings harmony into every aspect of life. This book is about inner action resulting from the inspiration arising from the wisdom already within the reader, which transforms self *(tikkun ha'nefesh)* and the planet *(tikkun ha'olam)*. It is not an attempt to prove a formula for peace.

What is meant by the word *peace?* Is it found simply by meditating in a cave? Is peace merely the absence of war? Will we obtain peace by preventing the destruction of the rainforests, by saving the whales and dolphins, by changing our economic or political systems, or by growing and eating only organic foods? The Sevenfold Path of Peace, based on the ancient teachings of the Essenes, takes us beyond narrow definitions of peace to a comprehensive and integrated understanding of the personal, social, and planetary dimensions of peace. Living this ancient, multi-leveled Sevenfold Path of Peace lays the foundation for the establishment of lasting planetary peace. This full peace is predicated on both the inner process of personal transformation and the outer process of planetary transformation.

The Sevenfold Path of Peace offers a modernization of ancient Essene wisdom so that we, too, can create peace within our lives, communities, and planet. This book is an expression of more than forty-five years as an active peaceworker from a variety of perspectives, as evidenced in the longer-than-usual biography, which shows the author is speaking from direct and heartfelt experience-based wisdom. The photos at the beginning of each chapter show the author in various expressions of the Sevenfold Path of Peace. Thus, this book is best experienced as a personal sharing rather than a documented essay with a lot of footnotes. To make the point that the ideas are more important than the supported "hard-fact" evidence, he has chosen not to footnote this book, but instead to give general references and reading for all the supportive information he cites. The real proof needs to be intuitively felt and then transferred into a life of living peace by being a feeling-based prayer of peace in every moment. *Creating Peace by Being Peace* is about becoming the essence of peace on all seven levels of one's life. It is not a theoretical spiritual discussion of peace or a single-focus approach. It is a framework for inspiring each moment into a living prayer of peace in a way that activates the expression of that living prayer in all of creation. Peace is the natural expression of the Culture of Life and Liberation; the experience of peace is part of our natural awakened normality state. You are invited to walk this Sevenfold Path of Peace along with the millions of people who already are. And one day may this planet be blessed that this humble path becomes a superhighway of peace, love, and healing for the world.

Blessings, Love, and Peace to you on this wondrous journey,

Rebbe Gabriel Cousens, MD

CHAPTER I

THE ESSENES AND KEY
UNDERSTANDINGS OF PEACE

A race by themselves, more remarkable than any other in this wide world.

Pliny the Elder

Indeed they are champions of faith, truth, and honesty ... as the servants and arbitrators of peace.

Josephus

WHO WERE THE ESSENES? The Modern Living Essene Way is a general path that resonates with the historical life and core truths of the ancient Essenes. It connects to the particular spiritual life of the prophetic, kabbalistic mystics of the desert, known as the Essenes. **It is a complete path and lineage of liberation that goes back 5,000 to 6,000 years, probably to the time of Adam, and more specifically was activated by Enoch, the seventh generation from Adam.**

The teachings and way of life of the Essenes were most accurately described by Flavius Josephus, the Roman historian, Pliny the Elder, and Philo, the Alexandrian philosopher. Others in this 300-year period refer to them, including Epiphanius, Eusebius, Hippolytus, Porphry, Strabo, and Chaeremon. Their information is supported by a number of modern historians such as Robert Eisenman, author of many books about these times including *The Dead Sea Scrolls Uncovered* (he was the one who forced the Dead Sea Scrolls to be released publicly and is professor of Middle East Religions and Archeology and Director of Judeo-Christian Origins at California State University) and Dr. Edmund Szekeley, who activated the Modern Essene Movement in the 1920s with his book *The*

Essene Gospel of Peace. There seems to be a general agreement among these historians on the uniqueness of the Essenes and the basic information about them. Dr. Szekely summarizes: "Among all the beautiful teachings known to man, none has had a more profound influence for good than that of the Essenes."

The Essene history documented by these historians covers approximately a 300-year span, from 186 BC to the destruction of the Great Temple and Qumran in 70 AD and the final Roman defeat of the Jewish people, including the remainder of the Essenes known as Zealots (those who would prefer to die rather than lose their sovereignty and be forced to live as slaves and prostitutes, denied their right to live in their spiritual ways by the Romans) at Masada three years later. This makes the point that there was a spectrum of Essenes. Some were married and others celibate; the typical Essene was a mystic of the desert, but others were called Zealots for their political translation of the scriptures into political action. Almost all were vegetarian, but some modern historians suggest that not all were. Some modern French archeologists have even hypothesized that Qumran was a spa at the Dead Sea. It is difficult to conclusively prove what actually was true 2,200 years ago, but the overwhelming evidence documented by ancient and modern historians supports these basic following statements.

Some of the great Essenes leaders known in the Christian world include Jesus, James the Just, John the Baptist, and John the Divine.

Josephus, after a three-year apprentice with them, described their teachings:

> The doctrine of the Essenes tends to teach all men that they confidently may trust their fate in the hands of God, and nothing happens without his will.
>
> They say that the soul is immortal, and they aspire to lead a righteous and honest life.
>
> They are the most honest people in the world, and always as good as their word.

They are very industrious and enterprising, and show great skill and concern in agriculture.

But most of all are those venerated, esteemed and admired who live in the wilderness.

On account of the sense of justice that they ever show and the courage and intrepidity that they manifest in ever defending truth and innocence.

They never keep servants. They do not think it is right that one should be the slave or servant of the other, as well as all men are brethren and God is their Father.

They also perform the service of priest and provide for all the wants, as food and clothing.

They all live the same simple, industrious, and frugal life.

The third class of philosophers among the Jews, and the class that is most esteemed for their just and moral life, is that of the Essenes.

They do not live in any particular town, but in every town the Order has its respective house . . . in every town is an Elder.

The Essenes' worship of God is grand, sacred, and majestic.

They eat and drink only what is necessary for their wants.

In general do they not act without the knowledge and consent of their elders. . . . But it is always left to their own free will to exercise benevolence and compassion to all in want, of all classes of society . . . to feed the hungry, clothe the naked, and shelter the homeless . . . to comfort the sick, and visit, assist, and comfort the prisoner . . . to comfort, aid, and protect the widows and fatherless.

They study with perseverance and interest ancient writings . . . they have profound knowledge of the art of healing, and study it arduously . . . they examine and are acquainted with the medicinal herbs and plants; which they prepare as medicine for man and beasts.

Robert Eisenman repeatedly points out they were coldwater bathers on a daily basis, wearers of only linen, and in general were purists in their life habits.

According to Philo and other authors of that time they were vegetarians (also confirmed by modern historians such as Eisenman) and took no drink other than rainwater or the juice of fruits. It is said that their diet was fruits, vegetables, nuts, seeds, and grains.

Others suggest they enjoyed music, dance, and other forms of movement and exercise. The Essenes were not seen as just philosophers, but were considered people of intense moral and physical action reflecting their intense beliefs.

In accordance with their lifestyle, outside of healing, they were collectively involved primarily in different forms of agriculture. As an extension of this, they discouraged living in cities. The Essenes were located all over the Middle East including the areas known today as Israel, Jordan, Syria, Lebanon, and Egypt. They seemed to be most concentrated around Mount Carmel, Qumran, and Lake Mareotis near Alexandria, Egypt, where they were called the Therapeutae.

> They are instructed in goodly books and the writings of the prophets and grow in wisdom and purity of heart.
>
> Many of the Essenes have often stepped forth among the people as prophets . . . their presages often came true, and this increased their esteem with the people as holy men and prophets.
>
> Rightly do they deserve to be called an example for the life of other people.
>
> Indeed, they are the champions of faith, truth and honesty . . . as the servants and arbitrators of peace.

With this historical understanding, the Essene Way is a potential bridge of spiritual unification, particularly for brothers and sisters of Jewish, Muslim, and Christian background who have a common father in Avraham. This bridge is sorely needed if we are to jointly create the preconditions of readiness for the Messianic Age. The preconditions are to wake up to the perennial truth of all paths: the Divine Presence is the essence of who we are. When we are in this consciousness, known as *deveikut* in the Living Essene Way, our essence is the truth of all religions. From that truth our natural state spontaneously emanates that noncausal love, peace, contentment, and joy we all seek.

The Modern Living Essene Way is not an attempt to go back to or mimic what we think the ancient Essenes were and did, but it is energetically aligned with these primordial energies. The Essene consciousness of deveikut, cleaving to God *(Yah),* implies constant communion with the Divine as an intense, overwhelming consciousness of the *Ein Sof,* or Divine Nothing—unmanifest as the sole reality. It is a comprehensive principle that relates to all that we are and do in this manifest world. It includes experiencing the Divine Presence in oneself and in all life. All life includes the four shamanic Essene kabbalistic categories of the living planet: *domem,* or rock people; *tsme'ach,* or sprouting people (plants or trees); *chayah,* or animated ones (animals, insects); and *m'daber,* or speaking ones (humans).

The Essene consciousness is that of the Awakened Ones. They are the ones who live in the Eternal Presence beyond the confines of the identification with the mind and body. Oral tradition says that Enoch, the seventh generation from Adam, who "walked with Yah and became whole," was the first Essene. Oral and written tradition also teaches that Enoch was taken up alive. Enoch then "walked with God and was no more" as he ascended as a fully God-merged being, and became Metatron, the chief archangel. Scriptures say that Noach also "walked with Yah and was whole." Noach's son, Shem, also known as Melchizadek, received the lineage from Noach and passed on the lineage to Avraham, who "walked before Yah and was whole." By walking before God, Avraham became a living blessing to the world. All those in the lineage of Avraham are considered of the Order of Melchizadek—*melchi* (king) or *tzadik* (holy person).

Certain oral tradition suggests the Sufis and the Essenes, who both suggest their mystical tradition of liberation goes back to Adam, may indeed have been one and the same mystic group at one time. The Essenes, in their most evolved inner spiritual circle, became the plant-based-only live-food Jewish mystical expression. The Sufis became the Islamic mystical expression, both knowing their essential oneness. Another essential link is that Ishmael and Yitzchak were the children of Avraham. This became more significant when Ishmael and Yitzchak came to peace at the time of Avraham's death; after Sarah's death, Haggar, Ishmael's mother, remarried Avraham after she changed her name and consciousness to Keturah. Their healing represents the potential and model of healing between the Jewish-Christian and the Islamic worlds. After the teachings of the lineage were transferred by Melchizadek (the son of Noach called Shem) to Avraham, they were then transferred to Yitzchak, to Yaakov, and to Yosef, and then reemerged with Moshe's (Moses') teachings of the first set of tablets brought down from Mount Sinai. In the Essene lore, according to scholar and Essene translator Dr. Edmond Bordeaux Szekely and kabbalistic oral tradition, these esoteric teachings, brought down by Moses, were given to those who were spiritually ready. But many of the people were not ready for these esoteric teachings of the tradition. The second set of tablets, containing what we call the Ten Commandments (Speakings), comprised the *exoteric* teachings given to guide the vast majority, who, in their spiritual immaturity, had created the golden calf. Until now, even the relatively concrete teachings of the magnificently simple and profound Ten Commandments have been too difficult for most of the world to follow.

The Essenes taught a way of being whole and peaceful that included following the laws of the Torah, but took one beyond rote performing of the laws. Their teachings were not meant to replace the Ten Commandments, but rather to offer a way to transform oneself into the living law of the Ten Commandments as the Ten Speakings. The teaching and lineage were given to King David, King Solomon, Samuel the Prophet, and to the prophets Elijah, Elisa, Isaiah, Jeremiah, Ezekiel, and Amos. Many of these prophets lived on the Mount Carmel mountain range and guided the people who gathered around them, creating a subtle beginning of Essene communities as far back as 600 BC. The initiatory prophetic mantra, according to the kabbalistic literature, was and still is *YHWH*. Although Gabriel did not have this information at the time when the Divine directly initiated him into the consciousness of the Tetragrammaton, he now understands that this mantra of the prophets became enlivened or awakened in him so that he might share it with others as an expression of the Essene lineage. It is likely that the esoteric Essene teachings were carried through the prophets on Mount Carmel and finally through the secret societies of the Essenes, who lived in communities three to six centuries BC around Mount Carmel, at Lake Mareotis in Egypt, and around the Dead Sea starting around 186 BC. The Essenes sent forth teachers from their own communities to share these teachings with all nations, including Menachem the Essene in 20 BC, John the Baptist, and John the Beloved, as well as Jesus, who is said to have been raised and educated in the Essene communities. Although it is difficult to absolutely prove that Jesus, Mary, and Joseph were Essenes, there is substantial oral and some written history that supports this. The subtle essence of the Essene teachings can be found in the beautiful Seven Beatitudes of Jesus' Sermon on the Mount.

Based on this information, and a document claimed to be found in the Vatican, the Romanian Jew, naturopath, scholar, and Renaissance man Dr. Szekely poetically translated the Essene Gospel of Peace in 1929. The power of his poetic and archetypical understanding launched the Modern Essene Way and inspired Gabriel. Through a 1995 revelation for the healing of self and the world, Gabriel was further inspired.

As the Essene tradition evolved, it touched many cultures. For example, in the sixth century BC, according to oral history of Pythagoras and oral Jewish history, he studied with the Essenes on Mount Carmel and came down both enlightened and as a proponent of live foods. The next mention of the Essenes is their evolvement from the Pious Ones. The Essene movement evolved from them into the Qumran community by the Dead Sea in 186 BCE. The Essenes were more complex and diversified than that portrayed in the Qumran community texts or by the Jewish historian, Josephus. Parallel to Qumran were the Mount Carmel Essenes and their communities, such as Nazareth in the foothills of Mount Carmel. This is where Joseph and Mary brought forth Jesus, or Yehoshua, who attained and taught the enlightened awareness of the Essenes. John the Baptist, also an Essene, was said to be the cousin of Jesus. The brother of Jesus, James, was Jesus' appointed successor, and he maintained the teachings of Jesus, including the teaching of good works and grace as foundations on the path. James also ran the Jerusalem church. All these spiritual luminaries were Essenes. This connection is the obvious meeting place between the Jewish and Christian worlds. Jesus taught the enlightened Torah and Talmudic prophetic ways of the Essenes as a Jew.

The Modern Living Essene Way represents the authentic historical teaching and practices of Jesus as it comes from his spiritual and historical context as an enlightened Essene, who many of the Essenes felt was the messiah of that generation. The teachings were that the messiah comes in every generation. Before Jesus was Menachem the Essene in 20 BC, who was also killed by the Romans. In 70 AD the Essenes dispersed, because of the Romans and the destruction of the second temple. The final mention of the Essenes was their valiant stand against the Romans in 73 CE at Masada (near the Dead Sea), where they chose "never to be servants to the Romans, nor to any other than God . . . and where they believed life without sovereignty was not worth living," according to Flavius Josephus. Except for a brief historical mention of Constantine—the Essene from Africa as a teacher in the Italian School of Medicine at Salerno, who taught Father Benedict, who saved Luigi Coronado's life by teaching him moderate eating—the Essenes were forgotten to history.

No one knows exactly what happened to the Essenes. In 69 AD, forewarned of the advancing Roman legions, they hid many of their manuscripts and sacred texts and seemed to disappear. Oral tradition suggests that they brought their teachings in small groups to the far corners of the earth. Some of them were said to have become Gnostics. Their knowledge has only resurfaced in this century through the finding of the Dead Sea Scrolls in 1947 at Qumran and a few manuscripts that had been preserved in monasteries. Some of these Essene manuscripts and fragments were actually found as early as 1897 by Rabbi Solomon Schachter at the Giza Temple in Cairo, where the author has visited. Some were also found in 1927 in the archives of the Vatican, at the castle of the Hapsburgs in Vienna, and in the British Museum by Dr. Szekely, who translated them into English. Many have called Dr. Szekely the first modern Essene. Through his wise understanding and efforts, the Essene teachings have again spread around the world. In 1929, before the Dead Sea Scrolls were found in 1947, Dr. Szekely reactivated the Essene energetic archetype with the Essene Gospel of Peace, Book 1. It is from this inspirational work that the Living Essene Way has blossomed. It is as relevant today as in ancient times. The essential Essene message of deveikut (God-merging), or "Walk before Yah and be whole," is an eternal spiritual message. To "walk before" means to be a blessing of God on this planet. Wake up and stay awake is the message and the blessing.

No historian can actually give us more than general information about what the different ancient Essene groups did on a day-to-day basis, but we do have significant knowledge of their historical and spiritual context (as described earlier), from which we can understand their fundamental spiritual path.

The general spiritual understandings given to Gabriel in a 1995 revelation were most likely followed by all of the Essenes regardless of their subgroup belief systems. To call oneself an Essene requires that one is aligned with the core-essence lineage of the Essene Way as it has been lived from the beginning of time, yet make it appropriate to our twenty-first-century lives. The Modern Living Essene Way revelation is about inspiration; it is not about judgment or living exactly as we imagined they lived in the past. It is about inspiring ourselves and others to live in the highest degree of peace and harmony with ourselves, others, animal and plant life, the planetary ecology, and the will of God in the twenty-first century.

Gabriel uses the phrase "Modern Living Essene Way" because our social-spiritual context and direction in these modern times is not identical to that of 3,000 or more years ago. Trying to adopt the rituals and lifestyle of those times is open to wide interpretation and potential self-righteous cultism. In the thirteenth century, the great Torah scholar, Nachmanides, in his introduction to the *Sefer HaMizvot L'Ha Rambam* (Book of the Commandments of Maimonides), spoke to this issue:

> I will not be for them [spiritual predecessors] like a donkey, eternally hauling their books. I will explain their teachings and study their ways, but when my vision does not complement theirs, I will decide according to what my own eyes are seeing and with legal certainty. For God grants wisdom in every generation and every period and will not deny goodness to those who are sincere.

The next evolutionary step in the unfolding of the Essene Way for the author came during July 1995, when the author did a twenty-one-day water fast. On the twenty-first day, over a period of six to twelve hours while meditating and praying in the temple at the Tree of Life Rejuvenation Center, he had a vision of the letters of the name of God, the Tetragrammaton in the form of Yod Hey Wah Hey, YHWH (That Which Was, Is, and Will Forever Be). The vision turned to flaming letters and burned themselves into his brain, third eye area, heart, and into every cell. They fully permeated every aspect of Gabriel's consciousness. YHWH is the vibration of the eternal, compassionate Divine Presence as it begins to manifest out of the Ein Sof (infinite-unmanifest). It was after this that the author began to speak in the third person to express the enlightened Essene teaching that we are not the body-mind-I Am complex, but that which is prior to the body-mind-I Am complex. This third-person expression and teaching of consciousness has also been used by such great Hasidic rabbis as Rebbe Zusha of Annopol, a third-generation Hasid in the lineage of the Magid of Mezeritch from the Ba'al Shem Tov, and by Rebbe Meir Premishlaner, another mystical and famous Hasidic teacher who was in the inner circle of ten of the students of the Ba'al Shem Tov, the enlightened founder of the Hasidic movement.

Over a continuous period of about six hours, while Gabriel meditated, he disappeared into the supernal light of the unmanifest and reemerged back into the flaming letters. Then the flaming letters of God's name began to symbolically talk to Gabriel. The four letters of the name gave different pieces of wisdom. It was not like channeling. The letters communicated directly into Gabriel's consciousness and what transpired was beyond the actual message. It was a total cosmic initiation and empowerment into the mysteries of the Tetragrammaton and the Essene kabbalistic Jewish lineage. It became, and is, part of Gabriel's soul essence in a way that cannot be explained, but can be transmuted energetically by touch, countenance, sound, or breath.

A portion of this divine communication has become a general template for the Modern Living Essene Way. The teaching is a modern expression of the historical Essenes, the shamanic, Jewish, kabbalistic, mystical prophets of the desert. The meaning and relevance of the Tetragrammaton that permeated the author's consciousness in the temple at the Tree of Life in 1995—in light of Gregg Braden's book, *The God Code* (2003)—takes on a more general message for creating world peace. *The God Code* articulates specifically how God's name (YHWH) reverberates in the DNA of all life. This teaching is also mentioned in J. J. Hurtak's earlier work, *The Keys of Enoch:* "The Name of YHWH is coded within every biochemical function in our body, especially within the life-giving DNA-RNA matrix." According to Hurtak:

> Every letter or combination of the divine code (YHWH) helps each individual to reprogram his or her own DNA through quantum coherence. Human consciousness infused into the golden ratios of DNA, microtubules, and clathrin molecules located as jewel-like geometries at the tips of microtubules, awakens and tunes the human body as a vibratory antenna, a virtual Tree of Life on a micro and macro scale!

This name of God is the activated energetic mantra in which Gabriel was initiated. As stated in Exodus (Shemot) 20:24, "... in all places where I cause my name to be pronounced, I will come to thee and I will bless thee." In other words, YHWH is the name of God placed in our minds and, thus, on our foreheads and in our hearts to draw grace. Further research strongly suggests it was also a mantra for meditation revealed to Moses, used by the prophets during their initiations to their students, and also most likely used by Jesus for his disciples. In this context, it is a uni-fying name of God reverberating in all creation as the name of God encoded in our human DNA, in the DNA of all living creatures and planet life, and in our hearts and minds.

The יה *(Yod Hey)* represents the balance of the inner female and male and the וה *(Wah Hey)* represents the balance of the outer male and female. In this context, it is a mantra of liberation of this lineage at least four thou-sand years old. This holy mantra *(hagiya)* can be used with the breath (Yod on the in-breath, and Hey on the out-breath):

> Yod into the Heart, and Hey out through the heart.
> Wah from the perineum area up to the third eye,
> Hey out through the heart.

This breath mantra is excellent for meditating and for maintaining a peace, love, and compassion awareness throughout the day.

In 1996, the following four principles of the Living Essene Way were recognized, acknowledged, and approved by all the main Essene groups in the U.S. at the Breitenbush Essene Conference. The four basic Essene principles are:

I. *Sh'ma Israel Adonai Elohenu Adonai Ehad*—God is One and many.

II. *Teshuva*—to return to God by changing one's ways to the ways of God; to know the self and live the way of God.

III. *Tikkun ha Olam*—to actively participate in the healing and trans-formation of the world.

IV. *Shalom*—the peace on seven levels, leading to ultimate peace of self-realization; peace that comes when we have integrated and unified our inner and outer worlds, balanced the inner and outer male and female (equality and respect between sexes), and created harmony between heaven and earth.

Four Main Principles of the Essene Path

I. *Sh'ma Israel Adonai Elohenu Adonai Ehad*—God Is One

Here we have the one God beyond time, space, and being, as YHWH means that which was, is, and will be. It is formless, neither male nor female. God is both transcendental and immanent. The point at which we experience the meeting of the transcendental and immanent is the personal experience of God. The Essene experience of God is the personal experience of the transcendental God concealed in the physical universe and ourselves. Once we discover the bliss of God in the universe, in ourselves, and in each other, God becomes personal and immanent. The gift that Avraham, our forefather, brought to us was not monotheism, but a personal relationship to the one God. This awareness is what has the potential to unify all people in the awareness of our one-soulness. The Modern Living Essene Way follows the example of Avraham, whose tent was open in all four directions, to serve all the people and share the personal, one God with all. Avraham's tent being open to all in all four directions is symbolized by the Maltese Cross worn by the Knights Hospitaller. Avraham was the living expression of the primary oral teaching of the ancient Kabbalah—to receive in order to share—and in that way expressed the loving energy of the Divine. His mission was *alma d'itgalia* (the revealed world), to share the teachings with all peoples and all cultures of the seventy nations, but in a way that all could hear them and incorporate the teachings into their particular culture. It is a teaching of universalism. It is the way of Rachel and her two children, Yosef and Benyamin, as well as that of his son, Yitzchak, and to a certain extent, that of Yaakov. It is the ability to hear the still voice inside, or as Enoch said in the Essene Gospel of Peace, Book 2, "Be still and know that I Am God (I Am That)," the foundational Essene message. God is a noun, not a verb. Yah is the unmoving absolute, which we may experience as the eternal unfolding of the Divine in our lives without beginning or end.

The Essenes were opposed to idol worship. They related to angels as messengers from God and carriers of prayers into the higher realms. They honored and respected angels but never worshiped them. According to the kabbalistic traditions, which were practiced and studied by the Essenes, creation started with the One and became the Many. The One is that which underlies and manifests as the Many. The Essenes saw themselves as working in cooperation with God, never as separate from the One, but as vehicles for the fulfillment of God's work of unifying the creation in the world of manifestation. The definition of idol worship is to give power to and focus on any thing as if separate from God, or an intermediary of God—money, symbols, physical idols, and so on. Even anger is a form of idol worship because it gives power to our anger as a separate source, rather than directly from God. The deeper teaching is that idol-worship takes us away from the mystical truth that God dwells within us, as us. Idol worship creates an illusion of duality that we are separate from God and God is outside of us. For this reason, idol worship tends to lose the mystical experience of our oneness as the spark of the Divine within us. In the Modern Essene Way, there is no intermediary between the body-mind-spirit complex (human being) and God. Idol worship limits us to the safety of worshiping the Golden Calf (that is, putting God in a box rather than going beyond the ego as Moses did in his walking up the mountain into the mystery of the Divine Self beyond the box).

II. Teshuva—To Return to God, and Live the Way of God, and Know the Self

Teshuva means to cling to or surrender to the way of God as it unfolds for us. It goes beyond the concept of repentance and practice of guilt. It is to be a vibrating, ecstatic vessel of God's light and will. Teshuva is about letting go of thoughts and actions that take us away from the presence of the Divine in our lives and to create thoughts, feelings, and actions that align us with the glorious experience of the Divine. Teshuva is to know the Self. It is living in the joyous experiential knowledge, wisdom, peace, and love of the higher Self. Teshuva means to refocus our priorities to live and eat in a way to enhance our communion with the Divine and to reconnect with the universal love of God's way. Teshuva means to return to God.

III. Tikkun ha Olam—To Actively Participate in the Healing and Transformation of the World

This principle means to create world peace by being peace.

The message of Moses on Mount Sinai was a call to ethical and spiritual freedom and liberation for all the people of the world. It is based on the fundamental understanding of oneness of all humans as one world soul and our interconnectedness with animals, plants, and all creation. At the same time it includes respecting and honoring the diversification of the "seventy nations" as taught in the Torah, so that all people may develop their own personal way of relating to the One.

One world soul or working in unity does not mean forcing anyone to follow one form of worshipping God. In this context, the Essenes have a special obligation to live in harmony with all creation and in accord with the transcendent unity view of the world. It is our work to share this unity vision, by example, with all sentient beings. The focus is not simply personal transcendence, but the social and spiritual transcendence of the whole world. It is bringing into the world a morality and spirituality that reflect awareness of the presence of Yah. It is the process of infusing the material world with a palpable spiritual presence. It includes surrendering to the will of God so we may become an expression of Yah's will on this planet.

There is evidence that the ancient Essenes actively participated in this universalist work of teaching the nations. For example, in 20 BCE, the Jerusalem Talmud recorded that Menachem the Essene, considered a messianic figure, led 160 Essenes to spread the Noachide "Commandments," or Utterances, to the Children of Noach. This is also why the author shares the Torah teachings relevant to peace; these teachings are to be shared with the world. They belong to the whole world. The Noachide Utterances are the seven universal sayings given originally to Adam, again to Noach after the flood, and repeated again as an intrinsic part of the divine revelation at Mount Sinai. They are recorded in the Babylonian Talmud, the Tractate Sanhedrin, and the Mishneh Torah of Maimonides. In this context, they are called the Path of the Righteous Gentile. The Righteous Gentiles are people of all different religious backgrounds and cultures who resonate with the source and the way of the covenant of the Seven Noachide Utterances. It includes those radiant souls who resonate with the Essene archetype and energies. The Noachide sayings are considered the most ancient covenant with Yah for establishing the foundation for living and rejoicing in the awareness of God's presence. According to kabbalistic teachings, the Righteous Jews, or Children of Israel, and Righteous Gentiles, or Children of Noach, will work together as equal partners in cooperation with God to bring about the healing and transformation of the planet and readiness for the Messianic Age. It is a partnership model with equal respect for all.

These seven Noachide laws are:

1. No idolatry. Idolatry is any service, devotion, or drawing forth energy, positive or negative, from any created thing with the attitude of worship, including angels, air, earth, fire, water, plants, stars, money, power, fame, and so on. It includes the worship of anything as if it is independent from God or an intermediary to God. The subject of idol worship is complex because all that is created is an aspect of the Divine. All is One. Therefore, all things with appropriate awareness can serve as a vehicle to connect with the One.

2. No blasphemy of God's name.
3. No murder.
4. No theft.
5. No adultery or incest (adultery in this biblical context means any form of sexual perversion, such as bestiality).
6. No cruelty to animals (this interpretation is compatible with the Essene ethics of the twenty-first century and the original ancient translation of this Noachide Utterance). This can be interpreted as a plant-source-only way of life, which by its very meaning eliminates cruelty to animals.
7. Establish courts of law to support people in the keeping of these universal laws. On a subtle personal level, it is not about judgment but rather implies maintaining the integrity of a state of noncomplicity and avoiding a conspiracy of silence with those who choose not to create alignment with these seven universal principles.

A person who follows these laws is considered one of the Pious Ones of the Nations. The seven Noachide Utterances apply equally to men and women. Those of Jewish origin are classically considered righteous if they follow all 613 Torah utterances given at Sinai.

The 613 utterances and the seven universal utterances are summed up by the prophet Amos, in Amos 5:4: "Seek [God] and live." An accurate paraphrase of this is "Walk with God and be whole," or from Genesis 17:1: "Walk with me and be whole." The revelation message that Gabriel experienced is the importance of knowing and understanding the framework of these teachings so we do not delude ourselves into thinking we are above these basics—that is a classical setup for falling out of alignment. In other words, no one is above honoring and respecting dharma, or right action, of the Seven Noachide Utterances or the Ten Utterances/Speakings (Commandments). Then, with the foundation in place, we can take the next step of rising above the mere following of teachings and ritual to directly know God and be whole. In this wholeness we actively unify the heavens and the earth in each moment.

IV. Shalom

Shalom is peace that comes when we integrate and unify inner and outer worlds, balance inner and outer male and female (equality and respect between sexes), and create harmony between the heavens and earth as a continual experience and feeling-prayer of peace, love, and compassion.

Shalom involves living and creating peace in every aspect of our lives, and on every level (the full Sevenfold Path of Peace) in order to prepare ourselves and the planet for the coming of the messianic energy, and to draw it here. It does not matter how one believes the Messianic Age will come, be it be through one person, through all, or a synergy of the two. What matters is that in this moment we actively live a lifestyle of shalom, which draws the messianic energy. A plant-source-only diet is an essential part of this way of peace. It is the dietary blueprint for the coming age of peace and is in alignment with the prophecy of Isaiah about the diet of messianic times being vegetarian. The fourteen Tree of Life Communions (which is not the same as the kabbalistic Tree of Life, which the Essenes studied also) and seven Peace Communions as outlined by Dr. Szekely are harmonic focalizers for the Modern Living Essene Way.

The fourteen Tree of Life Communions are divided into two sets of seven. The Seven Earthly Morning Communions are: Integration and Balance with the Living Planet, Top Soil and Power of Fertility, Life Force, Joy, Sun, Water, and Air. The Seven Cosmic Evening Communions are: Awareness of the Transcendental Self or I Am Awareness, Experiencing the Eternal in All, Right Livelihood, Peace, Power to Do the Will of God, Love, and Wisdom (the Ability to Distinguish the Real from the Unreal). Ultimate peace is the result of self-realization. It is living in continuous deveikut—full experiential consciousness of Divine Presence, prior to the mind. The communions support the quieting of the mind so that we can transcend the mind into the peace of liberation.

Three different ancient Essene teachings, from three ancient Essene teachers, are applicable to creating this peace. These teachings are levels of awareness, not techniques. They are shifts of awareness that allow one to perceive and react to all of one's life differently. When one imbibes these understandings, the Sevenfold Path of Peace and the Essene communions come to light and life in a completely different way. Life is fully peaceful. The first is from Enoch, considered the source of the ancient Essene movement. In the Essene Gospel of Peace, Book 2, Enoch says, "Be still and know that I Am God (I Am That)."

The second great teaching comes from the transmission of God to Moses as described in the Essene Gospel of Peace, Book 2: "I am the invisible law without beginning or end." The law, in this context, is the Tao. It is beyond good and evil. It is the living law of the heart. When people are not able to experience the living law of the heart, there is a need for the Ten Utterances as guidelines. By eating of the (kabbalistic) Tree of Life first and only then of the Tree of Knowledge (good and evil), we stay in the nondualistic awareness of that which is beyond beginning or end. When we are beyond time, we are beyond the time-mind-ego complex, which fills with guilt, remorse, resentment, loss of past, and anxiety, worry, and illusion of control of the future and even the present. The Eternal Presence of deveikut is beyond the mind and time. The Essene Way is to dance in the timeless joy, love, and peace of the Eternal Presence.

The third great teaching is from the Teacher of Righteousness (Essene Gospel of Peace, Book 2). It is a series of quotes complementary to each other, and, as the first two teachings, which express the Culture of Liberation.

> All the ills which men [and women] suffer are caused by those things without us; for what is within us can never make us suffer. Nothing real can ever be lost or taken away.
>
> **Essene Gospel of Peace, Book 2**

> All suffering comes from attachment, desire, and ignorance of what is real and unreal. Only That (God beyond time and space) is real; all the rest are just shadows. Everything outside of us is an illusion, for which we sacrifice our life force and consciousness to obtain, while

ignoring the great light within ourselves. "For to weigh thy happiness according to that which may befall thee, is to live as a slave. And to live according to the Angels which speak within thee, is to be free."

Essene Gospel of Peace, Book 2

The second quote elucidates the first quote, because the only way something outside of us can affect our peace is if it reverberates with some unresolved issues or negative thought forms in our minds.

In this doth happiness lie: to know what is thine, and what is not thine. ... And if thou dost desire and seek after that which doth not belong to thee, then shalt thou surely lose that which is thine.

Essene Gospel of Peace, Book 2

If thou wouldst have eternal life, hold fast to the eternity within thee, and grasp not at the shadows of the world of men [and women], which hold the seeds of death [a pre-dated allusion to the Culture of Life and the Culture of Death consciousness].

Essene Gospel of Peace, Book 2

Do ye not, then, barter that which is eternal, for that which dieth in an hour.

Essene Gospel of Peace, Book 2

THE ESSENE WAY OF LIFE AS A PEACE TEACHING

The Essenes practiced an agricultural, community-based lifestyle away from the cities. There were no rich or poor among them because of the alignment of their economics, lifestyle, and society with Divine Law. The Essenes considered Divine Law to be the sum total of all the laws governing all manifestations of the forces of nature and the cosmos. This Divine Law is perhaps best summarized as the Living Law of Love and Harmony with All Creation. In accordance with their sense of Divine Law, the Essenes had no slaves and were said to be the first society to condemn slavery both in theory and practice.

Although the Qumran Essenes lived in the harsh conditions of the desert, each person's material needs, food, and shelter were easily and abundantly met because of that person's alignment with the essential harmony of the universe. The Essenes were vegetarians; they avoided any form of alcohol except ceremonial wine; and they daily fed their bodies, minds, and souls with contemplation of the earthly and cosmic forces that they poetically called angels. They also worked with the traditional kabbalistic ten levels of sephirotic energies of the Tree of Life. In the morning they contemplated the forces (angels) of Nature. In the evening they contemplated the cosmic forces. At noontime each day they contemplated one aspect of the Sevenfold Path of Peace. Through this weekly cycle, the balance and practice of peace would be reviewed continuously. The results of this approach to life were extraordinary. In contrast to the short life span of the surrounding peoples, historians of the time have recorded that it was common for the Essenes to live to an average age of 120 years or more. *Creating Peace by Being Peace* presents this heritage of the Sevenfold Path of Peace as a framework for creating full peace in one's life. It is an approach for understanding how to create a holistic peace with the body, mind, family, community, culture, living planet (Earthly Mother in Dr. Szekely's translation), and the Radiant One (Heavenly Father).

Peace in the Modern World

The holistic approach of the Sevenfold Path of Peace often contrasts with what commonly happens among people working for a peaceful planet today. Many such people are working out of an intense, but single-issue, perspective. In the intensity of their effort, it is easy to forget, not acknowledge, or even be unaware of the other elements of the Sevenfold Path of

Peace. For example, after finishing a Tree of Life seminar in Anchorage, Alaska, the author attended the evening entertainment for a conference on bioregionalism and ecology. One of the lead speakers, who was more than a bit overweight, came onto the stage in an inebriated state. The author couldn't help but contrast the speaker's keen awareness and knowledge of bioregionalism and ecology with his obvious abuse and mismanagement of the immediate bioregion of his own body. In his inebriated state, he was hardly an example of a course of action that would lead to a balanced world peace. Our talk about world peace has little meaning if we are not willing to create peace in our own immediate lives the best we can, while at the same time having the compassion for ourselves and others as not perfect, as it teaches in the Torah, that none of the patriarchs or matriarchs of the lineage were perfect.

The author's interest in the Sevenfold Path of Peace came as a result of taking a hard look at the peace in his own life after many years of political activism. The author had worked with black teen gangs in Southside Chicago, on school health issues in Central Harlem in New York City, and on antiwar issues in San Francisco and Boston. He painfully realized that he, and most of his fellow social activists, despite high ideals and desire for social justice, had not attained any lasting peace in our own lives. What concerned the author even more was that activist approaches and tactics were not particularly different from those of the opposition, including the thought of being on the "right side." Like the opposition, activists were still operating on the principle that the "end justifies the means." Most of us, the author included, had been limiting ourselves with a narrow, self-righteous political focus that did not include the other six aspects of the Sevenfold Path of Peace. This single-view focus, while effective in a limited way, did not and does not create the overall harmony needed to achieve a life of total and lasting peace on either an individual or planetary level. After contemplating this distressing insight, the author dropped all outward political activity and went inward for what turned out to be a seven-year cycle of intense meditation, prayer, fasting, and other spiritual practices. He emerged from this cycle with an ongoing experience of the meaning of inner peace, or what some would call the transcendental peace of God. He was also aware, as his political efforts had shown him, that solely focusing on the transcendental self, and how wonderfully divine it is, could also lead to many imbalances. A wider perspective was needed, which his practice of the Sevenfold Path of Peace supplied.

Peace is not something that happens by accident. Peace is like silence; it is always there. The lack of harmony in our lives is like noise superimposed on the silence. The issue is not how to create peace, but how to live in a way that eliminates the noise.

Peace is not something we need to run away from the world to find. It involves us as fully mature and present human beings and requires of us a full, integrated relationship to the world on every level. Past Secretary General of the United Nations U Thant added to this understanding of peace when he said:

> Humans should have multiple allegiances: to oneself, to the family, to the culture, to the nation, to humanity, to the world, and to the universe.

The context for these multiple allegiances was clarified by Dag Hammarskjöld before he died:

> We have tried to make peace by every possible means, and we have failed. We can only succeed if there is a spiritual renaissance on this planet.

These multiple allegiances to peace are based on our direct, spiritual understanding of our inherent connectedness to all life. The Sevenfold Path of Peace is part of the blossoming of planetary consciousness as we flower into this spiritual renaissance. It is the ancient seeding the new. So, like the lives of the Essenes of old, our lives, nurtured by the understanding of the Sevenfold Path of Peace, can become spiritual testimonies to the total and lasting peace this world so desperately needs.

The Modern Living Essene Way

The Modern Living Essene Way, with its foundation in the perennial liberation wisdom teachings going back to Enoch, and perhaps even Adam, is not a religion. It is a way of life grounded by ancient and basic principles that can guide us to creating the Sevenfold Path of Peace in our lives, and on the living planet. The Essenes, like the Sufis, were the mystics of their respective traditions. According to oral tradition, they actually preceded these religions. It is possible that the ancient Sufi and Essene teachings have the same pre-Noachide source.

The modern Essenes represent, in the outer circles, an archetype of at least a plant-source-only and perhaps live-food diet—and for the inner circle, a liberation lifestyle of creating peace on every level by being peace on every level. Their communities were a crossroads for the mystics of many traditions to pass through, as well as being the historical birth energy and training ground/community consciousness in which Jesus, his brother James, and John the Baptist were raised. The point is that the Essenes represent an archetypical energy that is at the core of some of the great religions and wisdom traditions. It is the energy of the Culture of Life and Liberation in which the immanent and transcendent God awareness is the center focus of one's life.

The Essene Way is a way of liberation that goes beyond egocentric or ethnocentric to a world and cosmic-centric view. As we return to this core of ancient perennial wisdom, we can become inspired, no matter what our current religion, to begin living a lifestyle that creates peace on every level. One can live as an Essene no matter what one's religious preference. The Essenes represent a universal archetypical consciousness that can be lived in any context and not necessarily joined. If enough people choose to live this way, we can create an ever-widening circle of light and love among the cultures and religions of this world that will bring world peace.

A Lecture: The Essenes and Key Understandings of Peace

This section contains a slightly edited spontaneous talk given at the Moran Kibbutz in Israel in 2005. The author discussed the deeper causes of war and how to create peace. The lecture contains the essence of this book and gives a more personal experience of the author, as he spoke to a particular audience.

Creating lasting peace is about the merging of the heavens and the earth by being the living prayer of that peace. The heavens represent the soul and the earth represents the body. When we really get it, we get that the heavens and earth are already merged. That sense of duality that we create, thinking the heavens and earth aren't merged, is really what the work is. The new physics has already given us the answers that the spiritual philosophers are still struggling over. And what is that? We are all a bunch of biophotons! That's it. There's just one big field of biophotons that's beyond infinite, and then we particularize out of that. Yet, we're still biophotons dancing in the field. Does anybody know what a biophoton is? Truth is, we don't know exactly what they are, but their existence helps us understand this age-old dual/nondual discussion. Biophotons are subatomic particles that are infinitely in contact with each other. This means, when you tune into the field (we *are* the field, but when you tune into it, which means consciously connect with it), we understand all is in the field, and we understand our oneness, yet at the same time, we appear to be separate entities.

Even brain function—in which we think our brain is actually thinking—is a dualist illusion. What happens is, our brain is a receptor for the "biophoton Mother Ship." In this biophysic, quantum physic context, our brain and mind are linked with, and receiving information and energy from, the cosmos. We're all one; whether you call it dual or nondual it doesn't really matter. The real question is, since the heavens and earth are already merged, what's the problem?

The problem is that our perception is still one of separation. There are different ways that we do not have clear perception. For example, let's examine food from the point of view of the living field. The food we eat has a certain amount of biophoton energy, which is, in a sense, the radiations it gives off. Dr. Popp in Germany was able to show that the wild-grown food had twice the biophotons as organic, and the organic had five times that of commercial, and the cooked food had zero. He also showed that those who were healthy had higher biophoton radiation. This is measurable. The average junk-food person had about 1,000 units biophoton radiation. The average baby had about 43,000. The person who ate a good plant-based-only diet also had about 43,000. The average person eating live-foods had about 83,000. One person who ate live foods and wild herbs and fasted regularly had 114,000. What is the significance of this?

From Gabriel's point of view, what we see is, somehow along the line, the more live food we eat, the more biophoton energy we have, and biophotons communicate with other biophotons, which is something you probably haven't noticed—but the truth is, you have! Anyone who's been on live foods for a while feels more turned on. Raise your hand if you know what Gabriel's talking about [80 percent raise their hands]. That's all we're talking about. The fact is that the increased biophotons in our organism from the live foods are enhancing our conscious communication with the greater biophoton energy field in a way that we feel more conscious of it, when we eat at least 80 percent live foods. The field is always there. There are no directions and no goal here; it's simply to wake up to what's already there. We cannot attain what we already are. The good news is, we also can't lose what we never had. What we are doing when we're eating live foods is opening up the avenues of what we call "spiritual" connection to the greater whole, so we can more easily feel the oneness. Duality/nonduality—all that ends! We're just one. And in that one, there's the Particular (the individual body-mind-I Am complex called the personality) manifesting, and there's the Nothing manifesting. Not news—this is what the Kabbalists have talked about for years. The *b'li'mah*, the Nothing, and the *mah*, the Something—the b'li'mah and the mah. So, what's new? We think we're so smart, but really it is nothing new. We're just following up what people have known for thousands of years. We are that flame that burns as the dance between the b'li'mah and the mah. People are still arguing, "are we the nothing, or are we the something?" We're both simultaneously, and we always have been both simultaneously. Because our perception is limited, we don't get it, and we can only philosophize about it until we've had the direct experience. However, breaking through into this deeper understanding does get easier. This is the good news: it gets easier.

This is why we're moving into a new consciousness paradigm, because more and more people are getting it! More and more biophotons are communicating with somebody else's biophotons, and they're getting it! We're getting the truth. More people are awake today than ever before. Shanti and Gabriel just got back from Lebanon and Morocco. We were doing peace workshops and spiritual nutrition workshops. We did a two-day workshop in Lebanon. We had sixty-five people at the workshop in Beirut, and they would be completely comfortable sitting right here. Now, the newspapers may not let us think that, right? Mostly these people were kind of Christian-Yogi, but they would all identify as Maronite Christian. There is a split in Lebanon—they're not at war, you see—but there is a split between the Christians and Muslims. While, in Morocco, the different traditions respect each other, including Muslim and Jewish respect for each other. There are Muslims in Morocco who would be completely comfortable sharing this level of consciousness. Isn't that interesting? We're all sharing the same biophotons! There are people waking up all over the place. We're not talking about enlightenment, but just waking up to the truth that we're all connected. We have a Peace Every Day Initiative meditation group started in Beirut, one in Marrakech, Morocco, a minimum of four in Israel, and some in the U.S. It is really exciting because we're all in communication. There are over 175 groups around the world. We are all biophotons popping around in communication more and more. This is what the prophet Yeremiah said: "You shall know the Truth [some people say "Truth"; others say "Torah," or "Love"] in your inner hearts, and you'll know me from the very youngest to the very oldest." That's what's happening. We don't even have to try. We just have to be open. That's the good news.

The real issue is what keeps us from understanding we are all one big field of biophotons. This is a metaphor, of course—actually, it isn't; it's hard physics—but when Gabriel says "field" that makes it sound as if there's a boundary. But there is no boundary. It is infinite. It's really beyond infinite: *ein sof.*

So, what's going on? One way of looking at it is to say, let's identify with it. Why are some people waking up and some people not waking up? Why are some people still arguing about the nondual and dual? They've been doing that for thousands of years. Why don't they get the resolution to this question that has been asked for thousands of years? Why don't they get that we're just one big living field beyond dual and nondual concepts? When you stay at the mind, it is a cloud, because one cannot know God through the mind. When you go beyond the mind, then it gets very clear. We begin to see that the big issue is ego—which depends on the dominance of the mind over consciousness, and this clouds everything.

What's ego? In the *Sefer Yetzirah,* the first kabbalistic book, they looked at ego (and they didn't call it "ego" because they didn't have that term; they didn't speak English then and Freud had not manifested). Ego is equivalent to living in time and space and beingness. It's the total personality. That's ego. Let's understand that a little bit more now, because it's a key to understanding why we're resonating in love and light literally, all over the planet. There are people just saying, "Look, we're all one, why is all this fighting going on? What is going on?"

Let's start with form—also known as space—and look at that. There are two levels of form we can talk about. One level is the physical form, the physical body, and the other level is thought form. Both get us into ego trouble and start wars. How do they get us into trouble? Because we end up identifying with form, thinking it's us, rather than that we're consciousness manifesting as form. Whether it's a thought form or a physical form, it is still form. Wars based on religious differences are egoic thought-form wars. We can go right back to Israel, because we have to look here, we have to start with ourselves. We see, well, we have this conflict between the "religious" Jews, who think they have the right answer, and the secular, who may think they have an answer, and the spiritual, who also think they have an answer. But there's only one answer: *ayn zulato:* "There is only God."

Whether you want to call it dual or nondual, it doesn't really matter. It's missing the point that ego wants us to believe in our concepts and to identify with our concepts. Thought forms are also form and identifying with them is identifying with ego. We're so identified with our mental concepts and forms that we're willing to die for them! We're willing to hurt and kill other people for them. We have to be careful [about generalizing the Muslim world], since the Muslim world is very fragmented, like the Jewish and Christian world. There is no one monolithic Muslim, Jewish, or Christian viewpoint. In terms of who's what, clearly the Arab part of the extremist Muslim world certainly believes it's totally fine to kill anybody who disagrees, even other Muslims. This is what we see with the unfortunate Sunni-Shiite conflicts in the Middle East. It is this sectarian thinking that allowed the Sunnis to blow up the Shiite Golden Dome in Iraq, and the latent energy of a potential civil war in Iraq between Sunnis and Shiites. Where did that come from? Because people are so identified with their thoughts about who they are that they cannot possibly get that we're all one. This is the confusion caused by the ego.

Why are so many religions, nations, and tribes so identified with their thoughts? What a funny idea! What's happening is, the ego needs to feel good about itself, and it needs to feel it exists. For it to exist, it needs to identify with form, and it must maintain the form at all costs. That's the key to understanding ego. For ego to survive, you have to be either better or worse. You can be worse—that is, still an identity. Low self-esteem is just as good an identity for the ego as high self-esteem; it still is creating its existence. We identify with our ideas: "I believe in the nondual." "Oh, no, we're great individual expressions of the dual." People debate about these things, all having to do with being identified with a position. The point of liberation, and Gabriel has introduced the idea of the "Culture of Liberation," *ayn zulato*—there is only God—and there is no position to hold. The center point of the Culture of Liberation is that there is only God, and the point of life is to consciously merge with God. The only surrender, which is never to a person or a position, is to give up all positions. There is a place where there is no place to stand. This is what we're talking about when we talk about liberation: There's no place to stand, and you're free to move in whatever direction you'd like to go in. That's real freedom. Think about it—no place to stand! What is that like?

One thing that happens in the Culture of Liberation is we are certainly not going to be debating over concepts or belief systems, and we certainly aren't going to be going to war over belief systems. The Culture of Liberation is really what we're talking about when we're talking about Maronite Christians in Beirut resonating more with the people in this room than even those in this room with other people in Israel. And Muslims in Morocco resonating and being totally comfortable here, because they are sharing the Culture of Liberation, which is we're all one, and there's only God. *La'illa Ha il Al'Allah Hu* [a Moslem teaching]—there is nothing other than God. It doesn't really matter what terms we use; they're still concepts. Merging with God becomes the center of everything, the center rudder that guides us through life, guides us through our understanding. Life happens, but how we perceive what is happening is key. Knowing it all is a gift from God is the secret of peace. That's what opens us up to the biophoton field, and why other people are not able to open up because the wall of ego is so strong that it blocks the flow of consciousness. We cannot see what is going on. It gets humorous when you see it happening. It is really hard to think about wanting to kill someone else who makes a newspaper or magazine cartoon that you don't like. It's really hard to even grasp that kind of thinking, but that is what's happening. That is why there is war, strife, and difficulty—because the ego needs it. The ego needs to exist. It needs to be right. If it can feel separate, the ego is happy, because then it can have enemies, and enemies give it reason to make oneself better than, and make somebody else wrong, and the ego "you" keeps existing.

King Hussein II of Morocco, before he left his body in 1999, gave one piece of advice to his son, Mohammed VI. His son claims not to understand it. The advice was simply this, one word: "Survive." And that's the story of the ego. It has only one purpose: survive. If the ego can keep you from waking up, it feels it has to, because the minute you wake up it's out the door—that's the end for the ego! So, the ego works very, very hard to keep us identifying with form. Of course, we deal with it on physical plane because we have our concept of "more is better." "I have, therefore I am" is the mantra of the ego, and that's why money, power, and greed are dominant themes, because people are so empty inside (and not empty in terms of spirit, but empty because they're not feeling connected to spirit), that they somehow think gathering money and power is going to make them feel better. And it does for a little bit, but not for long. The mantra of survival is key to understanding this. "The more I have, the more I am" is an ego statement. It is a position on which wars are made. How many people with wealth say, "Yeah, I have the money—I make the decisions." Because that brings them to ego and brings them to power. They can't experience the truth because their ego will not allow them to. To experience the truth they would have to feel the biophoton unity that is existent.

The good news is, we are really waking up now. Has anyone heard of Rupert Sheldrake's theory of the morphogenic fields? Two . . . three. What Rupert Sheldrake from England theorized is basically the hundredth-monkey phenomenon. Whether that is a mythical story or not, what they report is that the monkeys on one island finally figured out how to wash sweet potatoes, and suddenly the monkeys on all the other islands spontaneously learned how to do it. That's it in a nutshell. What happened is they changed the morphogenic field of consciousness, and even though the monkeys weren't in verbal or physical "communication" because they were on different islands, they all got it. The morphogenic field is like a field of consciousness that people share, and that's the biophoton field. And as with us humans, this field now is starting to communicate. This is, for example, why it's possible that in 1987 at the Harmonic Convergence—does anybody remember that—we got together all over the world and meditated. We had 3,000 people meditating on a mountaintop in Sonoma County in Northern California. In a very short time, the Berlin Wall (the removal of which had seemed to be impossible) came down! There was a shift in the field. The Harmonic Convergence drew millions of people worldwide. Our group of 3,000 were chanting for twenty-four hours straight on top of this mountain. It was very nice; there were just thousands of people all over the world like us, and we collectively shifted the field. Can we prove for sure that the Berlin Wall came down because of that? No, we can't, but there was a feeling, because it was fairly directly related to that in linear time, that it did.

In the same way, world peace is a possibility for us if we shift the field. To do that, we have to understand our oneness, which is to really share. We have to go from a planet of receiving for self alone—which manifests as hoarding of resources and hoarding of food, resulting in an estimated 40 million people per year starving to death, and 29,500 children starving to death per day, according to the U.N. This results in obviously a great deal of pain and misery. These deaths from malnutrition are not necessarily caused by deficits in food production. If the world ate a plant-based-only diet (no flesh or dairy), there would be enough food to feed the world seven times over. Those are real shifts that are beginning to happen. This is laid out for us in the Torah. It's the Garden of Eden diet. So what's new? Is a plant-source-only cuisine a new idea? No, not at all—it is at least 5,700 years old, clearly stated in Genesis 1:29. But we're slow learners. We don't get it so quickly, but we're starting to get it! You know that there's a shift happening here, in this community. This is wonderful, and it's opening you up to the biophoton field, and what Gabriel has called the noncausal joy, the noncausal peace, and the noncausal contentment, which makes this whole process much easier. Because being awake and turned on is fun! This whole consciousness journey is fun. What makes it fun is we are able to identify more with consciousness than with form. That's really the key to the whole thing. What do you identify with? Are we consciousness? Or are we the form of our ideas? Are we the form of our belief systems? Are we our physical bodies? Are we a male or a female form, or are we consciousness manifesting—very different perceptions of how we live our lives. When we identify as consciousness, the power of the ego starts to fade away because it derives its power when we identify as form.

Time also identifies us with ego. Time has to do with being stuck in the past, believing in our stories of who we are. It also has to be going into the anxiety, fear-filled future. It puts us vulnerable to the idea of terrorism; terrorism only works if we're in the ego and we're focused on time. If we're in the presence, terrorism can't effect us. It would really ruin the day of the terrorists if everybody said, "Well, whatever. We're just being in the presence." There would be no power for them. They wouldn't be able to exist. They are, in a certain way, a really disturbed ego attempting to keep people caught in the ego. Terrorism keeps you in the fear and anxiety of the future, and keeps you from the truth, which is that there is only consciousness manifesting as the Divine Presence in this moment. "Oh, this happened to me, and therefore I can do this; this happened to me, and therefore I have a grievance." It then becomes a collective thing: "Well, the Israelis did this to us, and now we're going to do this to them." And the Israelis are thinking, "The Palestinians did this to us, and now we're going to get back at them." We have the tribal, collective ego-grievance that keeps war going, keeps conflict going.

Once we begin to understand these forces, and we don't identify with them, when people can be in the presence, we can start talking peace. One thing that is really nice about Hamas is that they're being very honest, which takes away all the confusion. Hamas is clear—[as of 2008] they actually still want to destroy Israel. Okay, at least we have an ego-discussion point here. We have a point of honesty. We cannot work out differences in any way without having some level of honesty. As a couples therapist, you can't even do successful therapy if the two people aren't being honest with each other. So, that almost brings us to a presence. It's not a presence that creates peace, but at least it's clarity. Then it allows some possibility of a direction and for creating peace. That direction involves breaking out of the ego-time-space paradigm of duality, and approaching the issue through the door of oneness (the nondual state). In this context, every Palestinian and Israeli killed is a part of our own soul and of the one world soul. Every death causes pain to our world soul, which *we feel* if we are tuned in to the world soul as our own soul. Perceiving the world from a place of unity, we are more likely to create peace. From a place of unity, it is possible to give up historical and collective vengeance and prejudices and come to a position of peace.

From the point of view of creating a sustainable peace, Hamas and Iran's honesty about wanting to destroy Israel or, at a minimum, remove Israelis from their Jewish ancestral homeland of 4,000 years, is at least a point of clarity. This doesn't, however, create a space of peace that validates the existence of the other. Historically, they are manifesting a feeling-thought form started by Mohammed in 650 AD when he killed all the men of a Jewish tribe in the northern Arab peninsula and sold all the women and children into slavery when the Jews of that area would not convert to his belief system (tribal ego structure). Instead of focusing on Mohammed's enlightened teachings, the terrorists' egoic mentality focuses on the culture-bound tribal egoic teaching of 650 AD. If we are interested in peace, it is time for an evolutionary update toward oneness and willingness for every tribe or peoples' right to exist away from tribal egoic domination and desire to exterminate those whose existence one believes threatens one's belief system. The egoic position "convert or be eliminated" given by Muslims to Jews and Christians, and by Christians in 1492 to Jews and Muslims, is evolutionarily dysfunctional—just as slavery, treating women unequally, and denial of civil rights are no longer evolutionarily acceptable. Now, at least there is some clarity for a sustainable peace. If we are to have world peace, all peoples and all cultures must have the right to exist. To do this, these groups need to let go of the outdated thought form of not acknowledging Israel's right to exist, which has been held as a tribal feeling-thought form for approximately 1,400 years and as a source of centuries of war and oppression. Ego creates war, both then and now.

Ultimately, when people are in the presence, there is peace. In the nation of Morocco, Gabriel had the opportunity to communicate with the head of Islamic affairs of Morocco. What is being shared in this talk is the same kind of discussion that we were having! We were totally in resonance, and so we'll probably do some peace work together. It's happening all over the world, and it doesn't break down whether you're a Muslim, or a Jew, or a Christian. Those are all identifying with forms. It's starting to break down as, "Do you get it? Are you open to the truth, or are you not open to the truth that we're all one? The struggle and stress over religious differences are ego thought forms." This is the key. If you're in ego, you need conflict. Ego needs conflict and dominance to exist. If you are in the presence, all time and form stops, and ego can't exist. We can see on a deeper level the motivations that keep the ball rolling toward negativity, conflict, and war: It's the ego's need to keep existing, and do whatever it can to do that, whether it's through time or form, including thought forms. In ego-time, it may be terrorism that keeps people in the fear-filled future, or historical collective national and tribal grievances against each other, i.e., collective thought forms. In basic ego-form, it may be "This is our land" and "No, it's our land." Religious ego thought form says, "Our form—our ego—must dominate over you because only we are right. If you don't agree with us, we have a right to kill you." This blatant ego position is the foundation for strife and war. Looking at it this way brings us into the evolution of consciousness that is slowly bringing us to the understanding that war is evolutionarily outdated and evolutionarily dysfunctional.

These conflicts go on that do not allow resolution because we are not thinking in the oneness. Our work as people who are beginning to wake up, and that includes everybody in the room, is that the more we identify with consciousness of oneness, rather than with time and space, the more we are beginning to create a collective vibration of peace. That's an interesting term. A collective biophoton communication where our biophotons are resonating with other like-minded biophotons, and it begins to spread out. Research for that has already been proven. In 1973 a study was done in twenty-two cities; the average city population was 25,000. In eleven of the cities, 1 percent of the population was meditating, and the crime rate became 16 percent less. They did another study in Rhode Island, which is a very small state. In Rhode Island they brought a few hundred meditators in, and the crime rate dropped 43 percent. Everybody said, "Oh, that's a fluke." So, they left, and the crime rate went back up. The next summer, they came back and did it again, and the crime rate dropped again approximately 43 percent. What was going on? We're simply enhancing our communication with the biophoton radiation and that energy. Everybody feels it, their biophotons kind of calm down, and violence diminishes. It's that simple!

In research done at HeartMath in California, they found that when you put DNA in a vacuum, it organizes the biophoton field. Just for background, DNA is considered the major transmitter of biophotons in the biological system. They also found that the heart, which is seven layers of muscle as liquid crystals, gives off a field that goes 5 to 8 feet outside the body. They also measured the field when people walked through the woods, they found that the field that was created was about 50 feet.

One of the other peace activities the Tree of Life sponsors is a peace meditation at each equinox and solstice at 7 p.m. The author used to lead these at the United Nations, as the Peace 21. We have gathered at each equinox and solstice since 1985. One researcher, over a period of more than four years, Buryl Paine, found that when people got together on each equinox and solstice, and did the meditation, the sunspots decreased 36 percent, compared to equinox and solstice times when people were not meditating. An increase in sunspots is connected with increase in emotional reactivity and disorder. The implication is that we are literally affecting the whole solar system by our collective meditation. So, we should not think we are powerless. We have tremendous power. What is the power? The power of our oneness. The power of our feeling-based prayer and meditation of peace, love, and compassion. The power of a small (unified) group as small as the square root of 1 percent of the population to start to positively affect the consciousness of the planet.

What happens, unfortunately, is about ten days after meditators leave an area, the crime rate goes back up again. We have to maintain the field, or chaos begins to happen, because the overwhelming energy of the global brain is fear and chaos; it is not yet unity, harmony, and love. Because of this understanding, we have created a Peace Every Day Initiative, saying, "Well, fine, let's just be a feeling-based prayer of peace, love, and compassion as meditation every day. This is not a big problem; let's just do that." That every-day feeling-based prayer and meditation is the commitment that has to happen if we're going to change the world.

The blessings of positive resonance cannot be activated if we are living in ego. The blessings cannot be activated unless the people are living the blessings. A message of the Zohar, roughly translated, is that when the people of Israel are able to overcome their ego differences and conflict with each other and live in oneness understanding, there will be peace in Israel. This peace will generate peace in the Middle East. This peace in the Middle East will inspire all the peoples in the world to move into oneness rather than ego-power-domination-hate consciousness, and there will be war no more. From Isaiah 2:6: "Spears will be beaten into plowshares." Our worldwide collective meditation, in which we link in a vision of world peace meditators surrounding the world beaming light onto the planet, empowers everyone to come into a collective consciousness of peace. This thereby supports all people to come to peace, including the peace that will activate the blessing of positive resonance among Israelis. There may be no peace for Israel until the people of Israel come into peace with each other.

We need to be really clear here. We are a long way from activating blessings of peace in Israel, the Middle East, and the planet because there is a tremendous amount of alignment with ego rather than the divine flow of God. There is the ego of identification with time, particularly with the ego state of revenge. Time is ego into the future, which empowers terrorism. Also there is the ego of identification of the I Am with form rather than consciousness. This kind of ego is identification of the I Am with the apparent separation of the different bodies, lands, structures, and thought forms. These identifications with form block the energy of peace.

You don't have to go too far to see the conflict between the orthodox, the spiritual, and the secular of the different cultures. And so, the work has to be done. The work is creating a biophoton field of peace to start communicating with the local and cultural brain, and eventually the global brain, to bring peace. It's work, but the work is really simple. We don't have to go out and confront anybody. All we have to do is get our biophotons in harmony. One research shows that in a chaotic field of 64 biophotons, if you get 8 biophotons in harmony, they'll bring the other 56 back into harmony. This is all we have to do. You could sit here in this room and meditate, and we could start positively affecting the consciousness of a government. We could start affecting the consciousness of the orthodox, secular, and spiritual people. We could start to melt the ego structures and ego identifications that are keeping people from having any sense of oneness. Does that not sound like fun! Doesn't that kind of bring a smile to your face?

So, it's really easy, and the more groups in each place that are doing it, we can change. A meditation group also did research in Israel. It was during the first Lebanese war, and the amount of violent incidents went way down when they were meditating in Israel. This is a small place—this is easy. If we have enough people doing this, we can make a huge difference. It needs some level of commitment. With this commitment on a worldwide basis we can change the consciousness of the world from hate and war to unity, love, and peace.

The feeling-based meditation and prayer is pretty simple. The theme is "one creates peace by being peace." We simply _become_ the vibration of peace: _l'hitpallel_ (become your prayer). How many people are familiar with that term? Good! The term means "to change yourself." That's what prayer is about. It's the absolute key to making this work. And so, what do we do? We go into the place of peace, which is really called meditation. When we are really in that place of peace, we simply feel our connection with all peoples (really all peaceworkers to start with), so we are affecting the global brain. We are communicating with other meditation groups who are working for peace in Israel, the Middle East, and the world—which is what we're trying to do. Then we visualize ourselves holding hands around the planet, generating light onto the planet, and the energy of love and peace. Then, become the living peace of the living planet. At the end, give thanks for this peace that has already happened.

The first big part is just getting into a place of peace, because again we have to create peace by being peace. That's just the basic meditation. There are different ways, and of course we will go over it and share the meditation here, this evening. Then Gabriel will take you through the last five minutes of it. We'll spend the majority of it just being in the place of peace. Then we'll take five minutes to consciously connect our biophotons out into the greater biophoton field, or living field. And it will work; some people think we need just the square root of 1 percent of the people meditating to change the planetary mind, the global brain. That's about 8,000 people, not a lot. Maybe we're going to need more; that's okay—we need more, we need more. Once it happens, that morphogenic field begins to move, begins to transmute. It begins to shift consciousness. And the more it happens, the more we start identifying with consciousness, rather than with ego mind as form and time! That's when the liberation begins to happen, and then the rest is grace.

The Six Foundations, as outlined and explained in the book *Spiritual Nutrition: Six Foundations for Spiritual Life,* make it easier to communicate at the biophoton level. The first foundation is spiritual fasting and spiritual nutrition. A diet for spiritual life is the Garden of Eden diet, which is at least 80 percent live, vegan, organic food made with love, high-mineral, low-sugar, not too much, individualized to our physical constitution, and spiritual fasting, which is wonderful to share with you and is excellent for quieting the mind. The second is building the life-force, the *prana:* yoga, pranayama, tai chi. The third is *sherut* and *tzedekah* (service and charity), which opens your heart up because when you give, it is a sense of connection. The Kabbalah teaches "Receive in order to share," and so it's playing out a deep kabbalistic teaching. The fourth is spiritual inspiration, which is what we are doing tonight, and a spiritual group, which is what this community is, for support, which is very, very important. The fifth is *kol demama* (divine silence), because it is from divine silence that all wisdom comes, and then *hagiya* (mantra repetition), *tefila* (prayer)—all these things create the divine silence. The sixth is *s'micha l'shefa,* or *hanihah,* Kundalini awakening initiation known as Shaktipat meditation. This is what we'll do tonight. The Six Foundations repair, strengthen, and open up the vessels as they quiet the activity and thoughts of the mind, and draw grace. But the Six Foundations are not practices; they are a way of life. They are ways of quieting the mind so that it is no longer an obstacle. When the mind is quiet we more easily begin to experience consciousness as our truth. When we're in the mind, when we're in our philosophies; when we're in our belief systems, the ego is very happy. The ego is *very* happy, because it knows that it's not going to die. Its ability to survive depends on our ability to keep fighting over concepts and ideas—but not about the truth. When we see the Six Foundations as a way of life, rather than as a technique or particular conceptual system, it allows us to simply live our lives in that happiness, in that joy, in that contentment, knowing that we are really not going anywhere. The Six Foundations create a peaceful mind, which creates a consciousness of inner peace. The Six Foundations dissolve our identity with the ego and create inner and outer peace. We already are that noncausal peace, but we just haven't awakened to that truth. As our biophotons become consciously aligned, we start to feel it more and more. From this inner place of peace, outer peace naturally arises. May the whole world be blessed with the seven levels of peace on a sustainable level.

Implicit in this lecture at the Moran kibbutz are several important principles that need to be clarified to understand how to create peace by being peace, which is the basic teaching of this book. A variety of research projects in quantum physics around the world, highlighted by a long list of contributors to the science of quantum awareness, such as Max Planck, Albert Einstein, Michio Kaku, David Boehm, John Wheeler, V. P. Poponin, Fritz-Albert Popp, Glen Rein, and others; visionary popular synthesis works by Gregg Braden and Lynn Taggert; and contributions from the ancient wisdom teachings such as Essene teaching—all confirm each other. They all lead us to the realization that we are all part of the living biophoton field, which is both the holographic container and the spark of God that exists in every part of all creation and that connects us all as one.

The holographic pattern that connects everything and is in everything appears to be the Tree of Life holographic pattern in the Essene kabbalistic tradition. It is found in all creation, from the macrocosmic to the microcosmic subatomic level. The living field is affected by and communicated to by the power of our feeling. Bodily experience, thought, and emotion create "feeling." Our feelings are reflected back to us in our lives through the mirror of the living field. Our inner feelings express their patterns within us by affecting and changing our DNA pattern. Research shows that these DNA patterns explicitly affect and reorder the outer biophoton field. This is how we as individualizations out of the living biophoton field affect the living field, the beyond infinite (Ein Sof). Research shows that our DNA vibration based on our emotions literally affects the whole solar system, as suggested by Buryl Paine in personal communication with the author, while monitoring Peace 21 meditations on the equinox and solstice. The research showed a 36 percent drop in sunspots (decreased sunspots are associated with less social chaos on the planet Earth) as compared to sunspot frequency on previous equinoxes and solstices when the worldwide Peace 21 group was not meditating. This was found to be true four years in a row.

This idea of complete teaching is implied in the first Essene teaching transmitted in Gabriel's Tree of Life temple vision, *S'hma Israel Adonai Elohenu Adonai Ehad* (listen, we are the many and the one). We can best communicate with this living field through the language of this living field, which, as the ancient Essenes taught, is through our inner feeling. Jesus revealed these teachings again, as reported in John 16:23–24, from the Aramaic translation:

> All things that you ask for directly ... from inside my name, you will be given. Ask without hidden desire or motive, and be surrounded by your answer. Be enveloped by what you desire, that your gladness be full.

The Essene Gospel of Peace, Book 4, says it summarily:

> First shall the Son of Man seek peace with his own body; for his body is as a mountain pond that reflects the sun when it is still and clear. When it is full of mud and stones it reflects nothing. Then shall the Son of Man seek peace with his own thoughts. ... There is no greater power in heaven and earth than the thought of the Son of Man. Through unseen by the eyes of the body, yet each thought has mighty strength, even such strength can shake the heavens. Then shall the son of Man seek peace with his own feelings.

We call on the Angel of Love to enter our feelings, that they may be purified. And all that was before impatience and discord will turn into harmony and peace. In Hebrew the teachings are translated into one word, l'hitpallel, which means to become our prayer. When we are in a state of inner peace, consciousness predominates over ego. When we are then able to focus conscious through the experience of our inner feeling we are able to communicate with and affect the living field. The only catch is that our internal feelings are always affecting the living field, either bringing chaos or elevated harmony and peace to it. This is why the Essene Sevenfold Path of Peace and the Six Foundations are so important, because they create a quiet mind in which the feeling of love and compassion are the carriers of our consciousness. Because we either consciously or unconsciously communicate with the living field, starting each thought and action with love and compassion is a powerful way to guide our feelings as they transform the field.

Another part of our communication with the living field, which empowers our effect on the living field, is to act as if it has already happened and be thankful for it happening. A concrete example of this whole process can be found in some Native Americans' tradition of creating rain by being rain. They imagine feeling the rain and smelling it, feeling the feet getting wet, sensing the change in the atmosphere, and further empowering the feeling by being thankful for it happening. It helps to remember that we are the miracle and that at this level we are no longer bound by the laws of Newtonian physics, as we saw with Moses splitting the Red Sea and Joshua ben Nun splitting the river Jordan. The theories evolving out of quantum physics do support this understanding right down to the vibration of our DNA. This supports what our modern quantum physicists have theorized, that the biophotons are in instantaneous communication throughout the universe as part of the living field. The implication is that our heartfelt meditations of peace create a feeling state of communication with the living field, and that creates less chaos and more harmony in the universe as far away as the sun.

Some key understandings and corollaries are associated with this. In the Essene secret teachings, we only pray for what we are already given, so what we pray for needs to be coming from an egoless place of service and fulfillment of destiny. As we activate our prayers by being them, we activate that same holographic pattern within everyone else and all creation. As a result, all of creation becomes a mirror of our inner feeling state. According to biophoton theory our inner state is instantly activated in the people around us and even the cosmos. The basis of the approach of creating peace by being peace is that the more people who are in a state of inner peace, the greater the overall holographic affect we are having in the participatory universe. The effect of inner peace begins to have a measurable effect when we reach the square root of 1 percent of the world population, or approximately 8,000 people. Realizing this should give all who are committed to creating peace by being peace a great sense of peace and joy. Gabriel speaks about this with great optimism because it means that with relatively few people we can begin to wake up the planetary consciousness to a world of peace and harmony, which is the holographic reality that resides in everyone.

So why is this so difficult? It has to do with the historical struggle within each of us between the Culture of Life and Liberation, and the Culture of Death. The Culture of Life and Liberation is represented by the consciousness of peace, cooperation, living in ecological harmony with the living planet by respecting the ecology, organic farming, eating organic food, using the power of natural healing with fasting, herbs, vitamins, creating happiness and respect in relationships, living by receiving in order to share, and acknowledging the spark of the Divine in ourselves and everyone else. The Culture of Life and Liberation emerges out of a God-centered, compassionate, and love-filled awareness that honors and respects all of creation. It is leading a life that is guided by consciousness rather than ego.

The Culture of Death is an ego-based view of how life is to be lived. It is a domination-centered way of life that often leads to war. Gratification comes not from the pleasure of God or love, but how effectively we can exploit the planet and other humans to gratify our material needs and ego desires of power and domination. The emphasis is on competition. It sees the living planet as resources to be dominated, hoarded, and exploited. Instead of health for the many, its focus is on wealth for the few, which leads us into disharmony with the planet and its resources; the living ecology is treated as a store in liquidation; the food-production focus is on pesticide- and herbicide-based farming, justifying that it is okay that those eating the agrochemicals may suffer from cancer and other forms of chronic disease from the toxicity because those in power have a greater right to make money than people have a right to a safe and healthy environment. This ego-based approach to global warming first denies its existence in the face of overwhelming scientific evidence to the contrary. Even when eventually the data is accepted by this ego-based approach, it fills the headlines with nice declarations—but little needed levels of action. This also reflects the attitude that the public domain such as air, earth, water, and sunlight can be violated for the principle that private enterprise is more important than the welfare and health of the public. This is in direct contradiction of the Essene and Torah teachings of valuing the public domain over private interests. It includes a pharmaceutical-based approach to life rather than one that naturally brings health and harmony. In the U.S., this has resulted in physician-based deaths, known as iatrogenic death or iatricide, having become the leading cause of death in the U.S., ahead of heart disease and cancer, according to *Death by Modern Medicine* by Carolyn Dean, MD, ND. This is the result of the "better living through chemistry" approach.

The Culture of Death has created its own set of ten commandments: (1) I am the center of the universe and there is no other God but me; (2) I serve only my ego gratification and needs; (3) I shall lie if it benefits me in everyday life and politics; (4) Murder is okay if it benefits my ego desires for power and manipulation; (5) Stealing from the masses is okay if it benefits my long-term and short-term ego desires and plans;

(6) Adultery is okay as long as my short-term ego needs are satisfied; (7) Gossip and public misinformation is okay if they serve my short- and long-term gratifications, political goals, and domination plans; (8) Manipulating the masses through fear-based crises are justified because my need for control and power is in the best interests of the masses as I assess their needs; (9) The truth on every level has nothing to do with everyday life; (10) All people and other living creatures, as well as the living planet, are mine to exploit.

CHAPTER 2

PEACE WITH THE BODY

Blessed is the Child of Light
Who is strong in body,
For he shall have oneness with the Earth. . . .
He who hath found peace with the body
Hath built a holy temple
Wherein may dwell forever
The spirit of God.

Essene Gospel of Peace, Book 2

Peace with the Physical Body

PEACE WITH THE BODY IS THE FIRST LEVEL OF AWARENESS. From the Essene Gospel of Peace, Book 4: "First shall the Son of Man seek Peace with his own body, for his body is as a mountain pond that reflects the sun when it is still and clear; but when it is full of mud and stones, it reflects nothing."

There are three aspects of developing peace with the body: (1) the body as its own ecological unit; (2) the body as a planetary cell in our global organism; and (3) the cosmic body. We'll look at all three in this chapter.

The Essenes perceived the body as the manifestation of the laws of life and the cosmos. They studied the body because they saw it as a key to the universe, following the principle "as above, so below." The body is the underlying functionality of the mind. So we think, so we feel. To find peace within our universe, within our community, and within ourselves, we must enrich the biological unit that houses our minds and souls. On this level, nature gives us seven healers:

- A functionally appropriate diet for the demands of daily life and for our spiritual life (ultimately, these are the same)
- Fresh air
- Pure water
- Adequate sunlight
- Exercise
- Rest
- Emotional, mental, and spiritual harmony

In our lives, we often become too busy working on our other projects to get the twenty minutes of sunlight we need each day, the pure water that once existed abundantly for all, the moderate exercise we need at least three times a week, unpolluted air outdoors, or adequate sleep and rest for our bodies. When we decide to commit ourselves to peace on every level, it is surprising how easy it is to create the time to make peace with the body. Without bringing nature's seven healers into our lives, it is difficult to discharge toxins from the body and allow the body to regenerate itself adequately. Consequently, our physical body slowly stops functioning in a healthy way and bodily dis-ease and disharmony begin to predominate. My experience is that it usually takes about two years to establish a stable program to maintain peace with the physical body.

Peace with the Diet

Developing an appropriate diet for all aspects of our lives is a complete practice on its own. To be at peace with the diet requires artful intelligence in combination with trial and error. It is important to realize that the exact diet for each person needs to be individualized with regard to the amount one eats, the timing of meals, and what one eats. A first step toward developing an appropriate diet is to be clear about the purposes of the diet. From the point of view of creating peace with the body, the main idea is to eat in a way that maintains and enhances the God communion in the preparation of the food, the eating of it, and the digesting of it. In *Spiritual Nutrition: Six Foundations for Spiritual Life and the Awakening of Kundalini,* the goal of eating was described as "not to live to eat, or eat to live, but to eat in order to enhance one's communion with the Divine."

A harmonious diet helps us honor, maintain, and purify the body as the physical aspect of the spirit and as the temple for the spirit in a way that keeps our minds clear and our bodies physically able to cope with the demands of our unfoldment. For example, if we eat excess sweets and throw our body out of balance into hypoglycemia, the unsteady blood sugar makes it difficult to experience sustained and deep meditations or to stay focused on a project. Blood sugar swings also contribute to periods of emotional lability, depression, or hyper-irritable states. We need an appropriate diet to help us assimilate, store, and conduct the heightened cosmic energies now being generated on this planet and to enable us to handle the intensified energy released through our own spiritual development. A diet that brings peace to our body supports us in all aspects of our lives from our physical work to our spiritual endeavors.

A plant-source-only cuisine is most compatible with the health of the body, mind, and spirit, as well as the health of the planet. Making a slow transition to a vegetarian diet is the most peaceful way to proceed. From the perspective of the Sevenfold Path of Peace, a harmonious process is more important than how quickly the goal is reached. Some people start by eliminating red meat from their diet, and then chicken and fish. Others start by observing one vegetarian day per week and increase the numbers of days until they get up to seven days per week. It is important to be gentle with yourself in making this change. Only set goals for yourself with which you will be successful.

A plant-source-only cuisine consisting of about 80 percent raw foods and 20 percent cooked foods adequately supports peace with the body. The author's experience, and according to some of the great nutritional teachers, such as Paavo Airola, PhD, Dr. Edmond Szekely, and the International Raw Food Summit of most of the leading vegan live-food teachers from around the world, is that this combination is generally the healthiest for optimal bodily function. The diet should include high-energy foods such as sprouts and freshly picked fruits and vegetables, some nuts and seeds, and grains and legumes. To help us let go of the inaccurate and fearful thought forms that cause resistance to such a cuisine, we need to recognize that the statistics from around the world overwhelmingly show that a plant-source-only cuisine is far superior to a meat-eating diet in terms of immediate and long-term health benefits and effects on longevity and physical endurance. As far back as 1917, research published in the *Yale Medical Journal* by Professor Irving Fisher showed that non-athlete vegetarians have about twice the endurance of athlete meat eaters. In 1961, the *Journal of the American Medical Association* editorialized, "A vegetarian diet can prevent ninety-seven percent of our coronary occlusions." In *Diet for a New America*, John Robbins points out that vegetarians who don't consume dairy products (vegans) have one-tenth as many heart attacks as meat eaters between the critical ages of forty-five to sixty-five. Vegetarians are even found to have fewer cases of anemia than meat eaters. The *American Journal of Clinical Nutrition* reported in its March 1983 issue that vegetarian women had less than one-half the instance of osteoporosis of meat-eating men. Researchers at leading research institutions such as Harvard and even the U.S. Department of Agriculture Survey on American Vegetarians have conceded that a vegetarian diet in advanced industrial areas such as the United States and Western Europe supplies more than adequate protein and meets all basic nutritional needs.

The Essenes intuitively understood what Gregg Braden's work pointed out, that the God Code is implanted in everyone. It is in everyone's DNA, from the plants to the walking beings, the flying beings, the swimming beings, and the human beings. That intuitive awareness from our own place of inner peace—which is true of the mystics of all traditions—brings us into a deep understanding of, and feeling of, great compassion for all beings because we understand our essential oneness. We understand that we are manifestations of the oneness into the world of duality. In that interconnectedness that we perceive, out of the inner understanding of our oneness, comes compassion and mercy for all beings. This is the paradigm of peace and of the Culture of Life and Liberation. The paradigm of ego, or the Culture of Death, as explained in the Author's Introduction, is one of an endless need to satisfy the ego by domination, separation, economic competition, exploitation of the environment, and aggression. This separation, which is the driving force behind ego and clearly an expression of a lack of understanding of our oneness, is played out in a variety of ways. One of the most important ways is in our dietary choices, which are reinforced in our consciousness for most people at least three times a day.

When we look at the issues of food, we have to look at where our dietary choices take us. From ancient times, we know from the Ayurvedic system, the Essene Way, and the Yogic system that what we eat affects not only the health of our bodies, but the essence of our consciousness. It affects everything from our mind and our thoughts, to our perceptions of the world, and our actions in the world. As we begin to look at issues of diet and a healthy body, we begin to have a very different set of perceptions from those which our current world believes.

"Our current world" means the last 10,000 years. Anthropologists have documented at least 3.2 million years of humans, in which the essential diet of humans was, in essence, the chimpanzee diet. The historical human diet is also similar to that of the bonobos, a very peaceful, friendly group of apes. What is useful to understand is that their essential diet—contrary to our myth of predator—was primarily a plant-source-only cuisine; the chimpanzees possibly eat a little flesh of occasional rodents. Dr. Robert Leakey, for example, points out that most likely, humans, as we see from a recent find of 3.2 million years ago, lived in trees and mostly like the bonobos, peacefully and communally. In other words, we weren't predators. The symbolic image of the caveman, pulling the woman by her hair, is an important image because when we understand the meaning of a dairy-and-egg diet, we understand that it symbolizes the oppression of the sacred feminine in the animal world. Humans were not primarily hunters. They were primarily gatherers.

When we start to look at this now, seeing the bigger picture, one archaic piece is common in many cultures: the myth that it is okay to exploit the female of a species. There was a time when even leaders like St. Thomas Aquinas said that women and animals don't have souls. Why did they say that? It is a justification to oppress females and animals. However, when we go back to the Torah, the Essene Way, the Kabbalists' teachings, the message is entirely different. It is that the breath of God was blown into all the animals first! All the living creatures came first, and the human came last. The kabbalistic implication is that the humans, coming last, incorporated the energies of all of creation. So we have within us those plant and animal energies of all of creation resonating in our DNA. That fits very much with the message of Gregg Braden's *The God Code,* that all life, from plant life to animal life to human life, has the same DNA code, which is Yod Hey.

As pointed out in the introduction, the currently activated articulation of the sacred name is Yod Hey Wah Hey. In the time of the messiah, according to the Essene kabbalistic tradition, the Wah Hey will be dropped, and it will be only Yod Hey. So, in essence, we are all sharing that code. In *The God Code,* it is Yod Hey Wah Gimel that really is in everybody's code in this moment. When we really wake up, it will be Yod Hey. When we follow the diet of Genesis 1:29, a plant-source-only diet, the dietary blueprint for creating the age of peace according to the Torah (Old Testament), and the world has shifted its perception and chooses to follow this diet, then we will evolve to the Yod Hey. Therefore, we will all be resonating at the same frequency. But now there is enough for us to resonate with; we have three fourths of the frequency (Yod, Hey, and Wah).

Once understanding this, we understand the shadow that has been created in our world. We are now being forced to wake up from our present dysfunctional cultural herd and herding mentality. Herding means a domination way of life; it is the essential expression of the Culture of Death. Before that we were gatherers. Prior to herding, found 10,000 years ago, the sacred feminine was very strong, meaning there was an acknowledgment of respect for mothers of all animals. In order to confine animals and kill animals for food, humans must go into a state of denial. The shadow must come so strongly that we cannot see the connection. The denial of living in the Culture of Death is so strong that our intuition is blocked. Herding consciousness takes us toward materialism, disconnectedness, and potential violence, which is the essence of ego. From the Essene point of view we use the word *satan*. Satan is not some guy running around with a pitchfork and a red suit. Satan is really the metaphor for the ego. It is an internal state. It is from that violence and materialism in which humans, as well as animals, are reduced to objects and products and valued by how much money they can make for those in power. The shift that needs to happen is just that: As we shift to a plant-source-only diet, we begin to shift to a diet of consciousness and Culture of Life and Liberation, away from domination and the Culture of Death.

We can look at this on different levels. One level is, as one of my teachers, Swami Prakashananda put it very beautifully:

> When we kill animals, we take in their fear, violence, and misery into us, and in us, it also causes fear, misery, and violence, which results in illness within us.

That level is called simple survival and is the direct karmic result of our actions.

On another level, as pointed out in *Spiritual Nutrition,* when we take death and misery into our body, we are affecting our subtle bodies, particularly what we call in yoga the 72,000 nadis and the central channel through which the primary spiritual energy of awakening flows, called the Kundalini. These nadis, including the central nadi, are disrupted and blocked by the energy of death and misery.

On a third level, beyond the individual subtle bodies, **eating meat and dairy is not only detrimental to personal health, but degrades the ecosystem.**

Eating flesh—more strongly than a plant-source-only diet—establishes us in the essential illusion that we are separate. This is a dual worldview in which there is no oneness—that animals don't have souls, and, if you take it far enough, that women don't have souls. These are the implications we need to truly understand of a flesh- and dairy-based diet. It is unfortunate that people have used the Bible to justify slavery by saying slaves don't have souls. This distorted thinking comes out of the shadow of death culture in which we want to believe these things, particularly when society is making so much money from it. Making money is a driving force behind the ego. Descartes' essential message was "I think, therefore I am." But the truth is "I am, therefore I think." The ego says, "I have, therefore I am." When we are not in a state of oneness, the I-haveness, which drives us into materialism, takes us into objectifying all of living creation and using it for product. Animals in this context become product, and in the herding mentality, humans may also become product as slaves. All the world has a potential of being enslaved by a few who have power, so that they keep building their ego, never ever touching into the truth. Once you touch into the truth, you understand that the herding mentality is the shadow of death and separation, and that we are truly one. Compassion comes from that sense of oneness.

On a fourth level, when we eat from nature, which was given to us for our survival and sustenance, we are imbibing all of creation, which is extremely powerful. When you eat from a fig tree, you are taking in all the cosmic energies that fed the tree—the sun energies, the earth energies, and the water energies. We are taking in the life force of all creation as we eat That and are filled by That; we are not taking in death. We are linking to the web of life in this dualistic plane. In our plant foods we take in the orchards, the fields, the forests, the cycles, the seasons, the energies of those who are organically farming and reaping with love. Sometimes people argue, "Well, plants have feelings." And truly, they do have feelings—we know this from the research outlined in *The Secret Life of Plants.* They do not, however have developed nervous systems as animals do. On a "bigger" level, the amount of food, such as the amount of grain required to produce meat, eggs, dairy, and farmed fish, is vastly more than that needed for the plant food, such as grain, directly. Thus a much lower volume of plants is killed to support a vegan diet than for a meat-centered diet. Ninety percent of the protein is lost when it is passed through animals, and 95–100 percent of carbohydrates and fats is lost. Flesh eating in this context is a hoarding of resources on all levels.

Fifty percent of all the fish that are gathered go to feed animals, which of course is way out of balance, especially since most of these animals are herbivores. Up to 80 percent of the grain that is exported from the U.S. is used to feed animals.

What does this mean? It means that today there is enough grain that would feed 10 billion people. But instead the grain is fed to the cows to fuel the flesh-food diet and not to the children. As Thich Nhat Hanh (author of *Being Peace*) said:

> If you do not eat mindfully, you are eating the flesh of your son and daughter, you are eating the flesh of your parent.
>
> Every day 40,000 children in the world die for lack of food. We who overeat in the West, we feed grain to animals to make meat, are eating the flesh of these children.
>
> **Speech at Riverside Church, New York, September 25, 2001**

Meat eaters are literally eating the flesh of these children. Why? The children are starving because the grain is being fed to the animals, and only those who can afford the much higher meat prices can eat.

We start to see connections that we don't necessarily want to see. This is why we cannot have peace until we have learned to intelligently see our shadow. When we shop for, prepare, and eat food, we need to go into denial about the suffering that's there when we're eating meat foods. We need to go into denial that we are disrupting the ecosystem, and need to be numb to the fact that we are destroying thousands of acres of land and oceans, and that as a consequence, our natural world is being destroyed. Every day, 25–30 million animals are destroyed to meet our food appetites. That's a lot of animals—a lot of death. One has to go into denial to consume that many animals. We need to look very closely at how we speak at the highest social-spiritual levels of love, kindness, freedom, and a gentler, kinder world, while our dietary actions are still those of violence.

It is helpful to understand that a plant-source-only diet as a support for peace is not a new idea. This connection has been made for thousands of years. We look back to Pythagoras, who lived around 600 BC, whose statements were very aligned with the importance of a plant-based-only cuisine as most supportive of consciousness and peace:

> As long as men massacre animals, they will kill each other. Indeed, he who sows the seeds of murder and pain, cannot reap joy and love.

Until 1850, when the word "vegetarian" was first used, people who were vegetarians or vegans were called Pythagoreans. The word "vegan" really wasn't coined until 1944 by Donald Watson, who made it very clear what the connections were. Quoting the *Articles of the Vegan Society of England:*

> "Veganism" denotes a philosophy and way of life which seeks to exclude—as far as is possible and practical—all forms of exploitation of, and cruelty to, animals for food, clothing, or any other purpose, and by extension promotes the development and use of animal-free alternatives for the betterment of humans, animals, and the environment. So, the word vegan includes protecting and respecting all sentient beings.

As Buddha said:

> If a man can control his body and mind and thereby refrains from eating animal flesh and wearing animal products, I say he will really be liberated.
>
> **The Surangama Sutra**

What this means is that one cannot hope to be liberated and be living off the flesh of sentient beings. This is the essential teaching of Buddha as well as the Dalai Lama, who declared he was becoming a vegetarian in April 2005, which should influence many, many Buddhists to move toward that goal.

The shadow of the Culture of Death is very strong. It is interesting that in the Buddhist tradition, the Jewish tradition, Christian tradition (Seventh Day Adventists, Unity Church, and early Christians), and probably all traditions but the Jain tradition, there has been a tendency to move away from the essential teachings of vegetarianism of the originators, who lived in that compassion for all creation because they knew their oneness from which the compassion grows. Rabbi Avraham Yitzchak Kook, first Chief Rabbi of Israel (called British Palestine in 1935, when he died), taught vegetarianism. We also understand from the Essene point of view that Jesus, who, as an Essene, taught not only the Ebionites but all his disciples about vegetarian way of life. In the book *Conscious Eating*, the author documented that all Jesus' disciples were indeed vegetarians, as well as were most of the leaders of the Christian church during its first two centuries.

It is important to understand that the early religious leaders really were more supportive of plant-source-only food for spiritual life. But then, as Moses Maimonides said, because people weren't really ready, they were allowed to eat a little bit of meat. Then, of course, people took it further, but vegetarianism was the essential teaching. For example, at the time of Jesus, moneychangers were changing money in the great Temple so people could buy animals to sacrifice, and that is why he disrupted the table. It wasn't because they were using money in the Temple—the teachings of the Temple were that everything comes from the holiness of the Temple. So all of the culture was coming out of the Temple, including the banking system, which would be essential if banking were to again support the Culture of Life and Liberation. Jesus' action was about disrupting the ability to buy animals to sacrifice. Part of the Essene teaching was and is that vegetarianism is a prelude to the Messianic Age. This view is also shared by Rabbi Joseph Albo (1380–1444) and indirectly by Rabbi Avaham Yitzchak HaKohen Kook (1865–1935), the Chief Rabbi of the pre-state Israel, who believed that sacrifices in the Messianic times would be only vegetarian.

From the point of understanding our essential DNA vibratory oneness, and going inside to feel that oneness intuitively in the silence in meditation, we come to compassion for all life. The next step is **ethical veganism.** This is not veganism because it is good for your health (and it *is* good for your health), or because it protects the environment (and it *does* protect the environment), but from a state of compassion. Protection of health and environment are more of a healthy survival level; they're more about protection and survival consciousness rather than the consciousness of spiritual evolvement. Both spiritual plant-source-only cuisine and ethical veganism are valuable, both are important. We are talking about a diet that leads us to quieting our mind, and then going beyond our quiet mind to our essential oneness. The loving-kindness that comes out of this diet, which creates peace, minimizes the suffering we impose on animals, humans, and biosystems. In this unity awareness, we are no longer egoic objects to be seen as commodities. When we are no longer being seen, or seeing others, as commodities, we are no longer forced to use cruelty to make the dominators feel good.

These are not new insights. These are insights that have been shared for more than 6,000 years. In fact, although many people don't really understand it, in the book *Conscious Eating,* the author outlines in detail how all the traditions essentially support a vegan way of life, or at least a vegetarian way of life. Some of the leading Muslim mystics, such as Rabia, were also vegetarian. M. R. Bawa Muhaiyaddeen, a great spiritual teacher in the Muslim tradition who lived in the 1900s, was a vegetarian and taught vegetarianism to his students. Some people believe that Muhammad favored vegetarianism. The essential question about diet and peace is where do we draw the line? It is in the spilling of blood. Who spills blood? We spill the blood of anything that has a smile on its face. Although we can say that what comes out of one's mouth is more important than what goes in, what we eat affects our consciousness and therefore what comes out of our mouth. By eating with compassion for all life—by not spilling blood—we positively affect our consciousness, and increase the power of compassion expressed by what comes out of our mouth. This is a huge shadow that we're dealing with, but it comes from the place of the ego that sees animals as objects to be exploited for food and money. The ego is about separation from all of creation. Acting out of the ego tears the fabric of oneness and harmony, and obviously our sense of peace, and creates a culture of domination. The early Native American cultures of the Great Plains, Bering Straits, and coastlines are an exception in that their hunting and killing was a spiritual practice of unity with the animal and not of herding.

Modern-day hunting of meat takes place mostly in a supermarket—which is an expression of domination not only of animals, but of humans by humans, because it is the same psychology. When we understand the psychology of ego, it is all about domination: "The more I have or dominate, the more I am." If I can conquer your land, the bigger I am, the better I feel about myself—at least temporarily. But it never works. It is always temporary because the ego is never satisfied.

Jim Mason, in his book *An Unnatural Order,* creates a strong historical link between the human enslavement of each other, and the human enslavement of animals for food. It is all, again, about the ego wanting domination. That state of peace that comes out of the state of inner quiet is difficult to have when one is eating death and cruelty, because it activates cruelty in the mind. Ramana Maharshi, a great Yogic saint, put it very nicely. When asked what was the best support to meditation and self-inquiry, he, a vegetarian, said "a pure diet." He said, "When you eat a pure diet, the thoughts of the mind become pure; they become quiet, and the knots of the heart become untied." That's what Gabriel is talking about. When we eat in a way that doesn't bring violence into ourselves, we quiet the thoughts of the mind and therefore are able to go deeper into meditation and therefore support our deeper insight of our oneness that comes from the place of enlightenment. At this level there is an intuitive insight of a oneness that leads us into compassion.

As we evolve in this way, we don't have to think about compassion; it evolves from our natural state. Our natural state is noncausal love, noncausal compassion (which comes out of the sense of love because love is the oneness), noncausal peace, noncausal contentment, and noncausal spiritual joy. Our natural state, which requires *no cause,* is what then creates a world of peace. **When we are in that state of essential peace, we can, by our actions, become a source of blessing for the world.** As Avraham was told by God, "Walk before me and be whole."

Transitioning to a plant-source-only cuisine helps us overcome social conditioning. Despite the Essenes, who are in a sense the spiritual foundation out of which Christianity grew, we know today that most groups of the Christian world, whose founders saw that vegetarianism was the appropriate dietary practice, are no longer following vegetarianism. For example, Unity Church founders Charles and Myrtle Fillmore were ethical vegetarians. Gabriel spoke at the Unity Church in Kansas City, and saw they were not vegetarians anymore! People said, "Vegetarianism is nice, but it's not essential." This also happened with Buddhism and Judaism (although Israel has the highest percentage of vegetarians outside of India). This is not new. It's not a criticism. It is saying people are affected by the domination culture that brings death, misery, and enslavement to all of creation. We need to appreciate that there is a constant shadow from the pervasive Culture of Death that is dominant in almost all societies on this planet.

The points that were just made have to do with the consciousness side of it. The other side is that indeed a plant-source-only way of life really is more healthy personally and ecologically. T. Colin Campbell points out in *The China Study* that a plant-based diet has by far a greater health benefit. Animal protein is, in essence, inferior to plant protein. This is not new information. The research also shows that a plant-based diet's protein, as pointed out in *Spiritual Nutrition,* also helps decreases insulin resistance. Without going into all the statistics, because that is not the point of this book, let it be said that a plant-source-only diet has significantly less heart disease, cancer, diabetes, kidney disease, immune disorders, and hypertension associated with it. This research is cited in *Conscious Eating* for people who want more detail.

Not only are we talking about herding of cattle, sheep, and goats; we're also talking about herding of fish. Half of the world's fish catch is fed to herbivores, such as cattle. The result is that all seventeen of our major global fisheries are depleted or in decline. The highly respected teacher, Rabbi Kook, said:

> Milk was destined to feed the animal's offspring, not that man should take it with force for himself. The kid has a right to enjoy its mother's milk and its mother's love, but hard-hearted man, influenced by his materialistic shadow outlook, changes and perverts these true functions. Thus this gentle kid is unable to partake of its mother's love and rejoice in the splendor of life.

The modern dairy cow lives three to four years, while the life span of a pre-tech, pre-hormone, pre-BGH dairy cow that is not having its life force milked out typically lived twenty-five to thirty-five years. On the Tree of Life website, we have detailed discussion about dairy—check out www.treeoflife.nu/why no dairy.

Dairy cows represent the feminine principle, as do hens. Both of them are systematically, technologically raped in order to keep their milk flowing and eggs dropping. They are chained or penned, and not allowed to act out their functions as mothers. Their babies get taken away from them. In essence, the feminine principle, or sacred feminine liberated, is completely dishonored in the way we treat hens and dairy cows. In essence, as one of Gabriel's spiritual teachers, Swami Prakashananda, put very clearly, we are taking in the vibration and energy of death, which affects us. We are affected because we become filled with the cruelty, violence, despair, misery, and the experience of enslavement these animals are feeling before they are killed. These creatures are deprived of the freedom to live as sentient beings; they are simply tools for making money. People, as they did during human slavery times, have "de-life-ized" these animals, taking away their souls, literally, by the way we treat them. We are participating in this when we eat these flesh foods. If we were not demanding them in the market, there wouldn't be profit in the deathly practices. The ego would be less interested, because the way it works from an egoic point of view is "the more I have, the better I feel." Therefore, if you have less because you are not making money from it, you would change, and the ego would move toward giving up the activity of a meat-centered diet.

The essential principle is that the ego necessarily creates a materialistic viewpoint when it treats all of creation, including industrial workers and really all humans, as commodities. The resulting separation and sense of disconnection keep us from understanding that we are, in essence, a unified field of consciousness manifesting as beings in time and space. This results in not only spiritual-vibrational pollution, but also in the death of about 25 billion animals, killed annually to support a flesh-centered diet and way of life. Every day we kill 25–30 million birds and animals, and 45 million fish. Our slaughterhouses kill approximately 20,000 land animals per minute. These energies feed our shadow. We have to work hard to deny it. We no longer need to be in denial; we can move on from this.

Ultimately, as we disregard the animal life, we create hardness toward all life, which then allows us to tolerate 40–60 million people starving to death each year, 29,500 children starving to death each day. It brings us into the constant war consciousness we are seeing all over the planet because we are in a constant state of desensitization. So, when we talk about peace, we have to understand that our meat-centered diet supports a mentality of violence, fear, slavery, and death.

This dietary reality has actually brought forth the four horseman of the apocalypse: famine, disease, war, and death. The four horsemen are not coming—they're already here.

As Ralph Waldo Emerson said, in *English Traits,* "The view of nature held by any people determine all their institutions." We have created a myth that we are predators; there's an extremely important implication to that. Rather than the view that our natural state is of noncausal love, noncausal compassion, noncausal joy, contentment, and feeling our unity, the myth that we are cruel, violent predators fuels our self-concept of who we are, along with our tendency to wage war. That's the ego speaking. That's what Emerson is talking about. When we create institutions that promote competition, cruelty, materialism, separation, and survival-of-the-fittest mentality. Our institutions represent and promote an ethical anesthesia. It isn't all from what we eat, but what we eat comes out of this illusionary cultural myth based on a sense of separation and lack of understanding that we are one vibrational DNA field manifesting as slightly different—but not by very much—variations of the DNA. Part of the creation of a Culture of Life and Liberation is to give up the idea that we are predators.

Isaac Bashevis Singer said:

> When a human kills an animal for food, he is neglecting his own hunger for justice. Man prays for mercy but is unwilling to extend it to others.

We *are* mercy; it is nothing we need to pray for when we realize it is our natural state. We have to change our life so we can live that way.

Environmental and Ecosystem Health

Our ecosystems are greatly affected by what we eat. Up to 80 percent of the grains and 50 percent of the fish are used to grow the billions of enslaved animals enough so they can be slaughtered. The estimates are that the amount of land, grain, water, and pollution involved to feed one human on a meat-based diet could feed fifteen on a plant-based diet. About 6,000 square miles of land are cleared every year to grow livestock—that's about 10,000 acres a day. It is just overwhelming what we are doing. We have reduced the average topsoil of about 20 inches to 6 inches. As described clearly in *Topsoil and Civilization,* no civilization has survived that has destroyed its topsoil.

Our streams are degraded by the tremendous amount of pollution that is produced by animal farms. As a result, 85 percent of U.S. freshwater resources are used up to produce animal foods. As pointed out in *Conscious Eating,* the average meat eater uses approximately 4,500 gallons of water per day, versus approximately 300 gallons of water for one living on a plant-source-only diet. One pound of California beef requires 5,200 gallons of water. Each pound of lettuce, tomatoes, potatoes, and corn requires 24 gallons.

The Use of Pesticides and Herbicides

According to World Watch Institute, about 1,000 agricultural pests are now immune to pesticides. Yet our shadow doesn't allow us to go back to the obvious solution, organic farming. At the Tree of Life we have worked out ways for a farmer to make a conversion to organic in one season's time with the use of micro-organisms. For topsoil to regenerate one inch naturally takes about 500 years. Our society's agriculture practice of growing grains primarily to feed animals creates an eroding of the soil at about thirty times the rate it takes to regrow one inch. Some 2 million acres are lost every year, and even more become depleted in minerals and nutrients. At the Tree of Life we have worked out a veganic organic farming system that actually adds minerals and rejuvenates the soil. We also have a veganic farming apprenticeship because it is so important these teachings get spread throughout the world. Vegan, organic agriculture is sustainable, while intensive commercial agriculture with pesticides and herbicides is not.

Energy Hoarding

The world is concerned right now about the use of petroleum. The energy ratio of petroleum input is twenty-two to twenty-seven times higher for one calorie of animal-based food than for plant food. We get upset because people are using SUVs; that's a ratio of 3:1 waste. When we look at the petroleum waste generated for chicken, fish, eggs, meat, and dairy products, the wastage ratio is 27:1! The shadow doesn't let us see this.

According to the U.S. Senate, the excretion waste from the animals on all these farms is 130 times greater than all the human waste in this country. This is important because the waste of these animals is far more toxic because of the misery, the violence, and their emotional state, not to mention the high bacteria, chemical, drug residues, and hormones that are in the excretory waste. One large pig factory creates more sewage than New York City! The enormity of this is amazing. New statistics suggest that 2.5 acres of land can meet the food energy needs of 25 people eating corn and cabbage, 15 people eating wheat, 2 people eating chicken or dairy products, and 1 person eating beef. These general statistics are available in a variety of books.

It is clear that not only does a plant-based diet increase our spiritual vibration rate and evolvement, and help our health significantly, but it would significantly reduce pollution of the earth and the waste of energy in a potentially energy-depleted society. We would reduce petroleum usage, decrease the amount of hydrocarbon and carbon dioxide that contributes to global warming, and, because of better health, save literally billions of dollars a year in medical, drug, and insurance expenses. The level of ignorance and denial about what is needed to sustain an animal-based diet, including dairy, eggs, and fish, is alarming. Letting go of an animal-based diet and shifting to a plant-source-only diet, we would significantly diminish the progressive extinction of species, rainforest destruction, air and water pollution, loss of water resources (50 to 85 percent of our water is lost or affected in some way by the animal industries), global warming, and dependence on foreign oil. We would also reduce disease, topsoil loss, drought, and forest fires, and reverse the rapid increase in desertification. It would also transition our consciousness more toward unity consciousness rather than egoic consciousness, and therefore decrease the need for war and terrorism.

A flesh-based diet is directly linked to the destruction of species and the ecology, violence such as war and terrorism, and separation consciousness. A flesh-based diet creates a hoarding of resources on every level, which increases the chaos and destruction in the world. A flesh-based diet is the diet of the Culture of Death; it feeds the ego of separation.

Conclusion

What we are basically looking at is our belief system of the Culture of Death, which is that we are egoic predators who can only feel better by enslaving or eating others from cannibalism to eggs and dairy. Our cultural belief system is very much affected by our daily practices. In the Culture of Life and Liberation, our meals are a celebration of peace. With a plant-based diet, we create a shift in the cultural consciousness toward peace. As Albert Schweitzer put it:

> We must fight against the spirit of unconscious cruelty with which we treat the animals. ... It is our duty to make the whole world recognize that.

Once we understand this ourselves, our work is first to live this consciousness, because we cannot share it without living it. When we live it and share it, we naturally begin moving away from the self-concept that we are ruthless predators. Significant research has shown the bonobos (a chimpanzee-ape-like species) are very peaceful, open, loving apes, whose diet is almost totally plant-based. The chimpanzee diet is also primarily plant-based. According to Robert Leakey, one of the most respected anthropologists in the world, the human diet was also primarily plant-based. Recent findings of human skeletons of 3.2 million years ago support Dr. Leakey's position that the ancient humans were primarily plant-source only. This information allows us to let go of our cultural myth that we are bloodthirsty beings who only know about domination, killing, and eating our kill. It means giving up the herding Culture of Death for one that is of gentleness, love, compassion, and respect for all of creation.

As almost all the teachings of all the traditions tell us, we cannot truly create happiness for ourselves if we sow seeds of misery for others. Some of the spiritual leaders who do not support killing of animals obviously include the Jewish-Essene-Kabbalist tradition's great prophets like Isaiah, Hosea, and Jeremiah, and St. Jerome, Clement, Tertulian, St. John Chrysostom, St. Benedict, and St. Francis in the Christian tradition. *Conscious Eating* also documents that there were the Christian vegetarian teachers of the eighteenth to twentieth centuries, such as John Wesley (founder of Methodism), William Metcalf (a Christian minister who wrote the first book on vegetarianism), Ellen G. White (founder of the Seventh Day Adventist Church), and Charles and Myrtle Fillmore (co-founders of Unity Church). Other vegetarian traditions include the Jain, the Sikh, Bahai, Catholic monastic traditions such as the Cistercians and Trappists, and the Greek Orthodox, who incidentally practice being vegan for 320 days of the year. In Zen tradition, the practice is called *shojin,* or religious abstention from food, and *ahimsa,* compassion. One Native American female shaman, before whom the White Buffalo Woman appeared, and who shared the essential tradition that she brought to the Western Plains Indians, explained that Native American tradition was to eat a plant-source-only cuisine, except during times such as winter when there is no other food available. Some research by Native Americans suggests that up to 60 percent of the Native Americans naturally ate a plant-source-only diet; they were primarily growers and gatherers, not hunters.

The teachings of the major religions support the spiritual and ultimately the cultural transformation that is associated with a plant-source-only cuisine, as this diet is an expression of a consciousness of oneness. When we reach this level war will be obsolete. Compassion, sharing a tribal understanding of our oneness, and uplifting each other will be more the paradigm of the Culture of Life and Liberation.

Yet we continue with our belief systems. As Voltaire put it, "If we believe in absurdities, we will commit atrocities." That is really what we are talking about, and that is really what is going on today. We pass those absurdities and atrocities from generation to generation. When we change our daily food way of life to one that reflects the consciousness of compassion, we obviously also change our personal lives and our culture in a direction that will bring peace. As St. Francis of Assisi put it:

> If we have men who will exclude any of God's creatures from the shelter of compassion and pity, then they will deal likewise with their fellow men.

It is a very straightforward connection. We need to see through our herding culture paradigm and our self-concept that we are violent predators. We are beings of peace. We always have been. Our essential nature is noncausal joy, noncausal peace, noncausal compassion, and noncausal contentment. This is something we discover when we touch in on the inner essence of who we are.

In essence, this way of life comes from knowing our oneness, manifested as compassion, manifested as a plant-source-only cuisine that helps to create a field of peace, love, and a sense of interconnectedness—otherwise known as world peace. The Culture of Life and Liberation manifests as a field of peace. Thoreau wrote:

> I have no doubt it is part of the destiny of the human race in its gradual improvement, to leave off eating animals as surely as the savage tribes have left off eating each other when they came in contact with the more civilized.

We are talking about becoming more civilized. That *is* what we are talking about. That will bring peace. It means letting go of oppression, gender inequality, violence, competition, and slavery, and moving toward cooperation, love, peace, and harmony. In essence, understanding our seed, which is our DNA frequency within all creation by the name of God, we then begin to plant these seeds consciously in all our actions. And from that comes world peace.

The bottom line is we can talk about this theoretically, but in fact we are what we eat, and every culture knows this. A plant-source-only way of life is a way of life that needs to be lived and not talked about. We must walk our talk.

We may hear something like, "Well, it is okay for you to live a plant-source-only way of life, but don't tell me what to do." This classical statement of the Culture of Death consciousness is in denial that our actions affect each other profoundly. A flesh-centered diet pollutes the rivers and lakes so we cannot swim or enjoy the beauty of nature. Our air and groundwater become polluted, which chokes off the four elements of air, earth, water, and sun (fire), needed to maintain viable life for all of creation. This air, earth, and water pollution poisons all of life, producing genetic mutations and the elimination of 1,000 species per year.

Money is taken from us through taxes to support ranchers, dairies, factory farming, feedlot operations, and predator-control operations. The forests that give beauty, maintain the soil, and support soil regeneration end up being destroyed to create room for livestock. Everything costs more, too, beyond the prices we see stamped on the meat in the grocery store. Our taxes support subsidizing animal agriculture. Medical insurance rates rise because flesh-eating employees have more chronic disease and weaker health. In Israel, there was an attempt to pass a bill that incentivized people to go vegetarian because a meat-based diet was costing approximately $35 billion a year in heart disease treatment. The bill did not pass, unfortunately, but its existence shows that even governments are beginning to understand this connection. So, when we talk about heart disease, cancer, kidney disease, diabetes, and obesity, we see that a meat-based diet greatly increases the health care costs shared by everyone. Our actions, on all levels, including our dietary choices, affect our human, animal, and plant neighbors now and in succeeding generations. Native Americans express this clearly when they share with the rest of the world, "OH MITAKUYE OYASIN"—To all my relations, which includes the rock people, plant and animal beings, and human beings.

The work of this book is obviously highlighting the negative implications of a flesh-centered diet on individual and world spiritual, health, economic, and environmental well-being, and all seven levels of peace. We would have better health, decreased demand for petroleum, and reduced use of antibiotic drugs and chemical resources because there would be less disease, restoration of millions of acres of land that would be available for agriculture, greater inner peace, and an elevation of spirit— this is very powerful for us to consider.

Where does the healing start? It starts in understanding we are one resonating DNA field. In that sense we have never been separate. It means rising above the egoic ideas of separation and our illusion that we are separate and therefore free to abuse animals and humans. Once we see that our role in life includes acting compassionately, to evolve spiritually, and to be a blessing to the whole world, peace with the body supported by eating a plant-source-only diet creates harmony on every level in the world. It is the expression of the inner truth of our oneness, of our resonating DNA. The love that comes from this understanding then brings compassion for all sentient beings. A plant-source-only cuisine is expression of our sense of interconnectedness and is the diet best suited for creating peace with the body and our world. When enough people have shifted to a plant-source-only way of life, then we will have created the preconditions for the Messianic Age because we will have created the preconditions of peace.

Peace with the Global Body

Most foods that are healthful for our individual bodies also seem to bring us into a peaceful relationship with ourselves as part of the planetary ecological body. Peace on one level often begets peace on another level. For example, a diet that doesn't require killing cattle, goats, sheep, chickens, turkeys, birds, or fish brings us into harmony with nature's universal law of love. A vegetarian is no longer directly participating in the creation of the suffering, pain, and death of animals on this planet. In the words of Jesus, as recorded in the Essene Gospel of Peace, Book 1:

> Kill neither men, nor beasts, nor yet the food which goes into your mouth. For if you eat living food, the same will quicken you, but if you kill your food, the dead food will kill you also.

The violence of killing animals for our dinner table rests upon the same foundation of "justifiable" violence that often leads to killing people.

As we begin to expand our understanding of peace with the diet and body to other levels, we see that it also links us with the planetary ecological organism. A full peaceful diet regularly honors our food as the main interface between ourselves and nature and brings us into harmony with nature and its universal laws. What we eat directly affects the problems of world hunger and global ecology.

Raising animals for the meat and dairy products at our dinner table has a significant effect on our ecological system. This process accounts for about 85 percent of the topsoil loss, and it consumes about one-half of the total water used in the United States. Livestock produce twenty times the excrement as the human population of the United States and regularly eat enough grain and soy to feed the U. S. population five times over. The total world livestock regularly eat about twice the calories as the human world population receives. It is ecologically shocking to realize (as pointed out by author Frances Moore Lappé in her revised edition of *Diet for a Small Planet*) that meat eaters require 4,500 gallons of water per day and three and one-half acres per year to produce the meat and dairy products they consume. People who consume a plant-source-only diet require one-sixth of an acre of land per year and 300 gallons of water per day to supply their food. In other words, fifteen people consuming a plant-source-only diet can live off the same land and water supply required to sustain one meat eater. Someone who doesn't eat dairy products or meat saves one acre of trees per year because of the smaller quantity of resources this diet demands. On our planet, with its ever-increasing shortages of land and water, this is a significant difference. The famous nutritionist Jean Mayer, in a U.S. Senate committee hearing in 1977, reported that if meat eaters were to cut their annual meat consumption by 10 percent, the 60 million people who starve to death each year could have adequate food. This doesn't mean that those who are starving would get the food. As Frances Moore Lappé, a founder of the anti-hunger organization Food First, points out, the basic cause of hunger today is a "scarcity of justice, not a scarcity of food." Hunger is a social disease.

As much as some of us would like to ignore it, what we eat affects the planetary organism. Although many of us have worked effectively for the survival of the earth, adopting a plant-source-only diet eliminates the level of contradiction between how we live and what we do beyond our personal lives to save the planet. According to the April 1990 *Vegetarian Times,* 76 percent of the U.S. population supports ecological action to save the planet, but only 2.8 percent are vegetarians. Sister Elizabeth Seton summarized our task nicely: "Live simply so that others may simply live." Because a vegetarian diet brings peace with the individual body and the planetary body, it is part of the blueprint for a peaceful planet.

PEACE WITH THE COSMIC BODY

On a cosmic level, the body is the vehicle we are given through which our thoughts, emotions, and feelings of love arise and take expression as a manifestation of Divine Will on earth. In terms of full spiritual development, honoring the body not only as the temple of the spirit but as the manifestation of the spirit leads us to what some call "full body enlightenment." Peace with the body leads us into the nowness of the physical state. The experience of peace with the body can be described as the awareness of a sense of full and delightful presence in the body. We spontaneously begin to have conscious contact with the energetic planes of our physical existence. When the body is in harmony, the subtle energetic flow of the cosmos can be felt moving through us in an exquisite, radiant, quiet ecstasy.

To be fully at peace with the body necessitates a perspective that we are not our body—that our body is a reflection of who we ultimately are on the spiritual level. This viewpoint motivates us to take appropriate care of our physical instrument, but not to fixate our ego on it. To know we are not the body helps us overcome our primal fear of death. Fear of death, ultimately the source of all fears, comes from our mistaken identification with our body. When the fear of death diminishes, then we can be completely at peace in our body. When fear fades, peace and love flourish.

Developing an appropriate way of life and diet in the context of an overall peaceful way of life aligns us with a greater planetary harmony. For our body to become a full manifestation of the spirit on this planet takes some time. During this transition, it is important to be at peace with and tolerant of the body, rather than forcing changes too quickly. This allows the transition to be made in a harmonious and peaceful way. With persistence and patience, most lifestyle and dietary changes to a plant-source-only cuisine can be made comfortably in the course of one or two years.

CHAPTER 3

PEACE WITH THE MIND

The crown of wisdom makes peace and perfect health to flourish.

Essene Gospel of Peace, Book 2

When this power [of thought] is guided by holy wisdom,
Then the thoughts of the Son of Man lead him to the heavenly
  kingdoms
And thus is paradise built on earth;
Then it is that your thoughts uplift the souls of men,
As the cold water of a rushing stream revives your body in the
  summer heat.

Essene Gospel of Peace, Book 4

PEACE WITH THE MIND INVOLVES CREATING A PEACEFUL MIND ON THREE LEVELS: the individual mind, or the totality of an individual's thoughts; the planetary mind, which is the totality of all the thoughts of all the individuals on the planet; and the cosmic mind, which is the totality of all of the cosmic thoughts in the universe.

Many people in our modern world suffer from a mind at war with itself. It is the author's observation, and that of the Essenes, that the mind tends to move toward a more peaceful state when we bring our lifestyle into harmony with the unwritten laws that govern the universe and human conduct. These laws can be found in the teachings of all the great scriptures. Love your neighbor as your Divine Self is a simple summary of the laws for human interaction.

PEACE WITH THE INDIVIDUAL MIND

Much of our lack of peace is the result of willingly exploiting ourselves by creating an overextended, imbalanced lifestyle organized around trying to accumulate what we often do not need and which is detrimental to our physical, emotional, mental, and spiritual well-being. This self-exploitation happens when we become ruled by our desires rather than controlling them. The result of this disharmonious state is that we lose touch with the very same peace, love, and tranquility that we hope to attain by fulfilling our worldly desires. The Essene Teacher of Righteousness in the Essene Gospel of Peace, Book 4, taught: "Do ye not, then, barter that which is eternal for that which dieth in an hour." Chinese philosopher Lao-tzu discusses another aspect of this human issue succinctly: "Without desire there is tranquility, and in this way all things would be at peace."

The author's experience, and that of many teachers throughout history, is that the primary method of controlling and dissolving the desires of the mind has been the practice of meditation on the Divine. Meditation eventually dissolves the desires of the mind that usurp our birthright of tranquility and peace. Prayer and a variety of other methods can also work. It is through the experience of this Divine Communion that we are filled with enough contentment, insight, and power to control our desires. The experience of Divine Communion puts us in touch with a sublime, noncausal joy (joy that comes without one's having to do something specific to create it) that *naturally* fills us with such peace that is the goal of all our desires. Then the need for peace and contentment is spontaneously fulfilled.

This inner contentment, which removes all desires, is one of the secrets of meditation. It is not that desires never arise again, but that we are no longer controlled by them because with meditation we can go right to the goal of our ultimate desire. In this state one can serve humanity without a lot of mental confusion. Meditation can create a perspective that also helps us get in touch with who we are and the best way to fulfill our life purpose on this planet. When the mind is clear, we are better able to direct the currents of emotion and bodily activities that move through us. Through meditation comes the realization that we are not our thoughts, or even our mind. It is possible to experience directly that we are the awareness that is beyond the mind. In this way, we develop an ability to witness our thoughts rather than become controlled by them. Through meditation, or other ways of working with the mind, we are also able to understand that the world is how we perceive it to be. If we perceive it through a filter of negative thoughts, we tend to respond more often to the environment in a negative way and thus amplify negative thoughts and experiences. Conversely, if we see the world through the understanding of the ancient wisdom that whatever God does is for the best, the same events are transformed into positive occurrences. After enough meditation, one develops the conscious power to choose naturally to see the glass "half full" rather than "half empty." In other worlds, the living field reflects back to us, our inner state.

Another silent source of mental unrest arises when we do not live in accordance with what we believe in our hearts. To continue to act contrary to our beliefs and not live and work in ways that we know will elevate us, slowly robs us of our life essence and meaningfulness. Living a life of quiet desperation does not bring peace of mind. The author is always impressed by the joy in people's hearts when they let go of what they think they need and begin to live in accordance with their own right livelihood and as the brightest light they can manifest.

Peace with the Planetary Mind

Understanding the planetary mind, which is the sum of all the thoughts of humanity, is a key to understanding the thought form for peace movement. All of our thoughts spontaneously add themselves to the planetary mind. Each individual's mind is affected by the planetary mind, so what we contribute to the planetary mind, positively or negatively, affects each one of us on this planet. The Essenes recognized thought forms or feelings as one of the most powerful forces on the planet. By taking responsibility for creating positive feelings, all of us, as individuals and even more so as groups of individuals, can elevate the consciousness on the planet.

Researchers such as Dr. William Tiller, former head of material sciences at Stanford University, have hypothesized that the power of the group feeling-thought form is equal to the square of the number of people in the group. This is supported by the understanding from Leviticus 26:7–8 that "one hundred will chase away ten thousand." Since 1973, many studies have demonstrated that when a critical number of meditators gather together to focus on the highest truth, there is a statistical decrease in the amount of social disorder in the area where they are meditating. The research cited in *The Maharishi Effect* points to a critical number to begin to bring about this social effect, which is estimated to be the square root of one percent of a population area. The profound implication of this phenomenon is one of the greatest hopes and potential power we have to create world peace. The proven power of group meditations has been a source of growth of feeling-thought form for peace movements such as: Creating Peace by Being Peace, which is a twice-daily, inner-feeling prayer and meditation experience; Peace the 21st, which encourages peacemakers to meditate for peace on each equinox and solstice at 7 p.m.; World Healing Hour, whose supporters meditate for peace at noon Greenwich time on the last day of each year; and a variety of other groups that suggest we meditate collectively for peace at 7:00 a.m. or noon daily, at noon on Sundays, or on the last day of each month. To practice this principle actively is a wonderful way to participate in creating peace consciousness on the planet. It is a way of healing the soul of the planet.

People's thoughts form a force field around them that transmits thought forms to the planetary mind. Our minds also receive feeling-thought forms from the planetary mind. We thus live, move, think, feel, and act in a planetary energy field. In a very concrete way, we are affected by the planetary mind whenever we turn on the TV, read the newspaper, or watch a movie.

Can we dispute that the Beatles, the *Star Wars* films, the *Star Trek* series, or Live Aid have had an effect on planetary consciousness? We are just beginning to recognize the impact of seeing people killed, shot, and tortured in our own living rooms on television. According to George Gerbner, who was a communications professor at the University of Pennsylvania and coauthor of the study "Violence Profile 1967–1989: Enduring Patterns," 70 percent of prime-time network programs use violence, and 90 percent of programs are violent during children's hours. Advertisements during children's programming hours have increased to twenty-five acts of violence per hour. The average American has seen 18,000 murders before graduating from high school. According to an Associated Press article of April 16, 1990, the American Academy of Pediatrics at its 1990 convention said that "long-term television viewing is one cause of violent and aggressive behavior in children." With the advent of various Internet video-sharing sites, it is now easier than ever to view real and fictional violence throughout the day. The violent thought forms reflected in the media cannot help but increase the violence in our society. This violence is a direct expression of the power of the Culture of Death. Peter Russell's concept of the global brain, which suggested that global mass communications would grow as complex and cross-connected as the human brain itself by the year 2000, further supports the idea that the creation of a tangible planetary mind is taking place, as we look at predictions for the world of 2008 as the power of the Internet expands, reflecting a neuro-active global brain. From the perspective of the Culture of Life and Liberation, it is our responsibility that our lives become expressions of living peace and we create or support media messages that generate a feeling of peace in our hearts rather than the holograph of fear, anxiety, cruelty, misery, and death.

The key question is, What is being communicated by this planetary mind? By creating a body-emotion-thought-feeling of a high vibration, we automatically help protect ourselves and others from the lower and chaotic vibratory thoughts of war, hate, jealousy, wasteful living,

excessive desire for wealth, and so forth. It has been my observation that by a steady practice of meditation, balanced living in harmony with the universal and natural laws, and a supportive social and spiritual system, we become increasingly immune to the negative thought-form forces that are being generated all over this planet. By adding thoughts of peace, we help to shift the planetary mind toward peace and the Culture of Life and Liberation, and away from the destructive state of the Culture of Death. The good news is that the cosmic laws of the living field suggest that we do not need majority to shift the planetary mind toward the Culture of Life and Liberation.

Peace with the Cosmic Mind

We connect with the cosmic mind when we create and live in harmony with the highest thoughts. The more we work in harmony with the cosmic mind and experience its manifestations in our surroundings and in our every cell, the more we become one with the cosmic mind. Often we start with a fleeting seed experience of the harmony of the cosmic mind. With practice, this awareness grows into a more steady state. The more we are able to communicate with the living field through our feeling state, the more effect we are able to have on the living field. We become conscious co-participants in shaping the living field. If we remain unconscious of our disharmonious thoughts or choose not to bring them into harmony, it becomes much easier to be affected by the overwhelming disharmony of the current planetary mind field. By unconsciously accepting disharmonious thoughts into our minds, we create an imbalance in our system. Based on the cosmic principle of like attracts like, any disharmonious thought we accept alters our own feeling state and creates a frequency that attracts other similar disharmonious thoughts.

The key understanding is that whatever our feeling-state prayer is—harmonious or chaotic—it will attract and set off a similar holo-

graphic pattern coming back to us from the planetary mind of the living field. One imbalanced feeling can end up attracting a whole disharmonious field of feelings within our feeling state. This disharmonious field then acts on the emotional body, causing imbalance on the emotional level. When both the mental and emotional bodies are out of harmony, we find that the physical body in turn takes on this disharmony as physical dis-ease. These disharmonies create a discordant physical, emotional, and mental DNA-generated field around the person, which affects the physical, emotional, and mental bodies of everyone else on the planet. Those closest to us are usually the most affected. This planetary imbalance may even affect other planetary bodies such as the sun. It is amazing how one negative, limiting, or disharmonious thought can cause such a mess. Like an uncontrolled mob, a disharmonious thought can become as contagious as a virulent virus. The good news is that a harmonious-compassionate-loving-peaceful feeling sets off a chain reaction toward harmony by attracting all the resonant harmonious feelings in the universe. This is how the Creating Peace by Being Peace way of life operates.

How can we make sure our thoughts are harmonious so that we don't create a cosmic mess? **One key secret to maintaining harmonious feeling is to start every thought with love, peace, and compassion. Love, peace, and compassion as the source of the first thought and word will shape the following thoughts, words, and actions.** Although there are a variety of ways to maintain this consciousness, the author has found that meditation and feeling-based prayer are two of the most powerful ways to maintain this inner feeling of love, peace, and compassion. By maintaining this inner state of love, peace, and compassion we become a constant living prayer.

From this inner space, we maintain a feeling-thought form of harmony that brings us into complete cooperation with the Divine Law. Through complete cooperation with the cosmic law, the inner holographic peace and harmony can be activated within each person on the planet. Peace through material, economic, or other technical approaches has not been, and will never be, enough to bring lasting peace to this planet.

CHAPTER 4

PEACE WITH THE FAMILY

Let thy love be as a sun
Which shines on all the creatures of the earth,
And does not favor one blade of grass for another.
And this love shall flow as a fountain
From brother to brother. . . .
He who hath found peace with his brothers
Hath entered the kingdom of Love.

Essene Gospel of Peace, Book 2

PEACE WITH THE FAMILY HAS EFFECTS ON PERSONAL, PLANE-
TARY, AND COSMIC LEVELS. It refers to the harmonious day-to-day
relationships with our immediate family, relatives, friends, and associates. When our own body and mind are quiet and at peace, we have peace
with ourselves and we more naturally express a feeling field of peace, love,
and compassion that has an uplifting effect on our family and immediate social environment. To love ourselves unconditionally gives us the
strength to love others unconditionally, and thus fulfill the teaching to
love our neighbor as ourselves.

Just as the individual thought body is the combination of all our
thoughts, so the individual feeling body is the cumulative field of all our
individual emotions. When bodily experience, thoughts, and emotions
are linked together, we create an individual feeling state. There is also a
planetary atmosphere created by the summation of all the individual feeling bodies on the planet. Every feeling we create sets up a resonance with

similar feelings in the planetary feeling body. Since the natural healthy function of the feeling body is to express noncausal love, compassion, and peace, when we give off these feelings we activate the holographic resonance of love, compassion, and peace of the planetary feeling body. Unfortunately, the opposite occurs when we create a disharmonious feeling. By virtue of the resonant field of the disharmonious feeling, we tune in to the force of all similar disharmonious feelings and attract that energy to ourselves.

This destructive force not only amplifies our individual negative feelings, but also directly affects the functioning of our physical bodies. According to the teachings in the field of psychoendocrinology, our emotional state affects the immune system. For example, when people are psychologically depressed, their immune systems also become depressed. As Norman Cousins's laughter therapy illustrates, the opposite is also true. A happy emotional state encourages a strong immune system. According to Dr. Szekely, the Essenes believed that allowing the feeling body to fulfill its true function, which is to express love, is the most powerful tool for creating health and joy. Epidemiological studies have shown that when there are tight-knit, supportive families and communities, the residents have lower incidence of heart disease and even live longer.

At one point in the historical evolution of the human race and, analogously, in our individual evolution starting from infancy, the instinctual and feeling body dominated our interactions. To be ruled by our emotions does not bring peace. It may even lead to a habitually reactive way of dealing with the world rather than an interactive way. Mob psychology is the extreme example of this. In the peace process, we make the transition toward creating a mature synthesis of our physical, emotional, and thought bodies. Our wisdom mind is given the power to focalize our emotions and bring harmony and integration for all three bodies. This doesn't mean that we aren't in touch with the full range of our feelings. It means that our actions on a personal and planetary level are going beyond an acting out of our primitive or impulsive emotions or desires;

we move from a reactive to a proactive level of interaction. Peace Pilgrim, a woman who walked across this country for decades spreading the message of peace, put it nicely: "If we were mature people, war would be no problem; it would be impossible." To be mature, from the point of view of peace, means to live with an awareness of love and tolerance, which harmonizes with the wisdom of our intellect. In this context, suffering is caused by desiring anything other than God. When we extend this principle of the personal ego's desire-suffering cycle, we can see how a collective attachment on a national level may lead to a blind nationalism, which in turn leads us into war in order to satisfy a national ego. This sort of uncontrolled national emotional body has created much planetary suffering throughout history.

Families exist not only for propagation, but also to provide a training ground for learning how to develop intimacy and a mature emotional body. This function is true for all long-term relationships. Life in the family is designed by its very nature to help our feeling body mature. **Intimacy is one of the last frontiers of human consciousness. In true intimate relationships, one experiences durable love, steady trust, and a willingness to be vulnerable. Durable intimacy requires a continual willingness to keep one's heart open under any circumstances. Intimacy is not about having a fixed and secure relationship. It is about being willing to leap into the unknown with your intimate other; it is about being willing to face all the issues of the human condition with one's partner, from birth to death; it includes healing the patterns of one's family of origin. Relationship in this context is not about shaping a partner into your idea of who he or she should be, but supporting the partner in reaching full potential as a mature and aware human being. It is about helping your partner be the full wild woman or man each of us is meant to be. At the highest level, each inspires the other to move deeper into unity with the Divine.** In this way, a durable commitment to intimacy in relationship is a powerful spiritual path. This is also the key to developing a loving relationship. When we have developed a mature feeling body, we are able to love without controlling or being controlled. We are able to love out of choice and not need. This is not "love as a business deal," which involves subtle and not-so-subtle levels of co-dependency such as "You love me, and I love you," or "You give me what I want, and I give you what you want." Mature love means loving from a noncausal source in which your personal love enhances the basic experience of love. If one is established in the inner state of noncausal love, compassion, and peace, it is difficult to slip into a state of un-love and alienation feelings of "You don't love me," and other aspects of a closed heart frequency that create disharmony in the feeling body. As a result of a body that has become a vehicle of light, and a heart-mind that is in the bliss of noncausal love, one is never dependent on one's partner for the experience of love, and his or her love does add to the joy and strength of the experience. The most direct way to know love in every moment is to be love in every moment rather than to demand it from someone else. One of the teachings of peace with the family is that real love cannot be demanded.

For most people, the ability to be love in every moment comes from creating a constant communion with the Divine One, the One who is ever present on all levels of our existence. Those of us who choose to take the risk of nonmanipulative, open-hearted love draw love spontaneously to ourselves. Those of us who are constantly searching for love usually do not find it until we, ourselves, become immersed in love. Love does not stop when we are rejected or seemingly not loved; it stops when we withhold love from another or forget our connection with the Divine.

One of the hardest practices of peace with the family is to keep one's heart open in every situation family life creates. It means, for example, that as parents we do not succumb to the temporary urge to close our hearts when our teenage children go through their rejection rituals aimed at making us feel unloved, unneeded, and unappreciated. As a parent of two, the author has found that an open, although sometimes wounded, heart eventually wins over teenagers' love because it preserves their sense of being loved. When a teen can't create rejection in us, love remains. The author's marriage relationship has been a great source of spiritual maturity because we continue to challenge each other in the context of consciously maintaining open-hearted vulnerability. This is a powerful practice. Through the experience of an ever-blossoming marriage and as a family therapist, one sees that when people have the courage to love each other in full, vulnerable intimacy, without holding resentments, their relationship will work out to its highest potential. Love in the family brings peace.

There is a deep and wonderful secret to this. It is the power of blessing, and the prayer of seeing beauty in all of life. The awareness of beauty is more than a perfect visual moment such as a perfect sunset. It is a soul-deep feeling-experience of the beauty in all people and in all situations, including one's "mundane" daily interaction with spouse and children. Sometimes, in the midst of some activity, Gabriel will turn to Shanti and share his experience of her beauty. This recognition usually changes the moment and is a reminder of the sacredness of our relationship and the moment. It is developing the inner eye that experiences perfection in what may appear as an "imperfect person or situation." In kabbalistic terminology it is the practice of *azamara,* or seeing the spark of light in all things and situations. We are not creating an illusionary spark of light but are seeing the beauty or spark of light that is already there, which we had not previously recognized. Once we have found one spark of light, it opens the door to seeing even more sparks of light as beauty in a person or situation. What opens us up to the beauty in all situations is to be living in the constant feeling-prayer of beauty. Applying this prayer of beauty in our personal relationship brings extraordinary effects of love and maintaining an open heart of love. In our personal relationship Shanti and Gabriel are always celebrating our prayer of beauty with each other. When one sees the beauty in another, it becomes the mirror of the living field reflecting that beauty and love back to you. It is an extraordinarily delightful way to live and celebrate the Divine Presence in all people and situations.

Another general secret for maintaining an open heart is the power of blessing another person or situation that one may perceive as hurtful. The blessing is not about blessing the other (as there is no other); it is about momentarily opening the heart so that we can move into the witness awareness and see the hurt, past or present, as a temporary misperception, which we can then release rather than remain stuck in as a point of pain within our psychosomatic structure. The power of blessing is the power to change our life and in the reflection, the power to change the life of the illusionary other that appears in the living field as something separate from our individualization. It is in the family that we have the opportunity to learn the power of blessing and prayer of beauty in a direct and daily way. It becomes obvious that this family experience becomes the model for creating the beauty and blessing of world peace. The power of blessing and vision of beauty through the feeling-based prayer that is our feeling in every moment not only changes us, but creates a reflective response in the world of peace, love, compassion, and beauty. The family remains the unit of physical and spiritual health as it is our primary training ground in the living of feeling-based prayer. Yet, even without the advantage of the primer of family training we have the holographic awareness of blessing, beauty, love, compassion, and peace within us that is able to be activated by those in this wonderful world who are being the prayer of blessing, peace, love, compassion, and beauty. We then become the change that we would like to see in the world. Each moment is the expression of our living prayer. Our life becomes the prayer. Our prayer is who we are. Our living prayer is a healing message to the living field for the healing of disease, dysfunctional family and couple patterns, difficult interpersonal situations, and the war and domination energy of the Culture of Death.

The ability to be insulted without retaliation creates peace in all sorts of human interactions. For example, about twenty years ago after presenting some peace proposals at a school board meeting, the author was bitterly and personally attacked by a religious anti-peace group for "being a meditator, and for promoting peace in the schools." After the meeting, he wrote a letter to one of the people who had attacked him, making it clear that the only way he could deal with the nature of her attack was to forgive her completely. She responded beautifully, and we were able to establish a friendly and respectful dialogue. This reinforced the meaning of the words of Jesus, "Love thy enemies." The truth is that loving our enemies means we have no enemies; love turns them all into friends. To love and forgive in this way is a wonderful practice that brings peace to every aspect of family and community life, and it is the bedrock for creating a world family. The way of peace is the way of love. Forgiveness is the way of love.

Behind the effort of loving fully is the inspiration of Divine Love, which is both the result and the cause of the ability and courage to love. Communion with the Divine sustains us in the state of harmony and love with our family. Love of the Divine is the ultimate source of a harmonious feeling body and peace with the personal and planetary family.

When there is peace with the family, when we have achieved some degree of love for ourselves and love for those in close relationship with us, then it seems almost natural that we begin to move toward peace with humanity. In England in the 1930s, a unique ten-year study on what contributes to health was carried out at the Pioneer Health Centre; it was called the Peckham Experiment (described in detail in *The Peckham Experiment* by Innes Pearse and Lucy Crocker). It involved more than 5,000 families. This study found that the unit of health was not the individual, but the family. In addition, when the health of the family was in jeopardy, the individuals tended to withdraw from social engagement outside the family. When the family health was strong, the individual members would participate more actively in the world outside the family. Loving family relationships are an important template for how we function in the world community. The great Chinese sage Lao-tzu put it nicely: **"The wise accept all people as their own family."**

An example of how peace with the family could work in the current world affairs would be a specific application for the Palestinian-Israeli lack of peace. As both peoples are the children of Avraham, and respect for the family is important in Middle Eastern Avrahamic culture, a sign of a heartfelt move toward peace would be to release the majority of political prisoners from Israeli jails. There are an estimated 11,000 to 12,000 political prisoners and many are connected to families of eight to ten people. The author's experience is that the Palestinian family structure is very strongly felt. Such a recognition and support for family life by returning fathers and sons and mothers and daughters to their families, once they have signed a declaration of peace before release, would create a potential heart opening and beginning of forgiveness in the hearts of some 100,000 Palestinians. It would create a moment of blessing and beauty to help repair the torn fabric of this relationship. Of course, there is a tendency for these former prisoners to return to their former anti-Israel activities, so it might include only releasing those who acknowledge the right of Israel to exist and who commit to work nonviolently for peace, and releasing these individuals in a gradual fashion to make sure this compassionate approach does not backfire.

This kind of sincere heartfelt action of supporting family life could be more powerful than talk about peace. The author speaks as a grandfather, father, and son. A way to peace is acknowledging the right of all families to exist in their intact form. Creating conditions that support love and health in a family supports the opening of the energy of love in many places. **Creating peace in the Middle East is not simply about political maneuvers; it is about supporting love in family life for all families.** Love your neighbors' family as you would love your own. A unilateral move, not simply a political prisoner exchange, but to support family life, could be very powerful. In the same level, in 2007, more than 2,000 Kassam Rockets have been fired from Hamas-run Gaza into bordering Israeli towns and the Negev, distinctly disrupting family life in those areas. Stopping continuous rocket attacks and suicide bombings, as well as returning kidnapped Israeli soldiers such as Cpl. Gilad Shalit, as a sign of goodwill would certainly show a respect for Israeli family life and create a more sincere mood conducive to serious peace negotiations. These are not solutions for a lasting peace, but represent some heartfelt first steps for the inner healing that is so desperately needed.

THE PLANETARY FAMILY

The belief that we are all one family is not simply a New Age idea. Its roots can be traced back at least as far as the Torah (Old Testament), with the Hebrew tribe's belief that peace between people is one of the foundations of creation. According to the commentary of *The Torah Anthology* (published in 1730 by one of the great sages of the time, Rabbi Yaakov Culi), the Hebrews were referred to in the plural until they received the divine guidance of the Torah on Mount Sinai. Once they were spiritually unified through the Torah, they were referred to in the singular. When they lived in unity, they were considered as a single soul. Lasting peace on this planet will come when we experience all the people of the world as one soul.

CHAPTER 5

Peace with Community

There shall be no peace among peoples
Till there be one garden of the brotherhood
Over the earth.

Essene Gospel of Peace, Book 2

PEACE WITH HUMANITY IS THE ULTIMATE RESULT OF A SHIFT IN INDIVIDUAL CONSCIOUSNESS TO THE AWARENESS OF GLOBAL UNITY. Peace with humanity is harmony between groups of people on a social, economic, political, and spiritual basis. It is the culmination of the collective process of individuals who are at peace with themselves and have shifted into unity consciousness. It is a shift from family, tribal, and national identities to a global identity as one people. To accomplish this, we must break our habitual identification with what Alan Watts called being "skin-encapsulated" entities, seeing everyone outside of our own skin as different, separate, and foreign. This fractionalized, alienated attitude of perceiving ourselves as separate from the whole may be healed by seeing ourselves as part of the whole. The more we meditate and try to live in harmony with natural and divine laws, the more we are likely to experience this oneness. Peace with humanity includes planetary systems of justice that are respected and a planetary economy that is designed to create peace and meet basic needs for the many rather than unbelievable accumulation of wealth by the few.

In *The Global Brain,* Peter Russell hypothesizes that the escalating pace of planetary communication is resulting in an ever-increasing shared awareness of international interconnectedness. For the first time in history, we are able to use this planetary communication to have regular, simultaneous global peace meditations, such as Peace the 21st and the World Healing Hour on December 31st, as well as musical events for peace such as the Concert for Bangladesh and Live-Aid. For the first time in history, almost all of the planet has direct access to spiritual teaching from past to present. Because of increased international travel, general international turmoil, international corporate activity, and the psycho-spiritual interface of East and West, we are beginning to experience the world as smaller and more unified. The Internet has accelerated the ease of global communication, and although the Culture of Death sometimes seeks to suppress Internet connectivity, such as in the violent suppression of the Buddhist monks and the Burmese people in late 2007 with its concomitant shutting down of the Internet, the creativity of the people in creating an unstoppable communication network will further assert our oneness—and no suppressive government will be able to prevent it. We still have a long way to go in this transition to a full sense of global unity, and a corresponding absence of an "us and them" mentality. But this will surely happen as the global brain process unfolds and expands. The increase in international travel has also helped to break down the walls of separation resulting from lack of familiarity. One of our roles as peacemakers is to help give birth to this evolutionary step.

Humanity has never experienced full peace in any age in history because there have never been enough mature individuals who were willing and able to live according to natural and divine law. The rich and strong have almost always exploited the poor and weak, economically, socially, religiously, and politically. Great wealth is concentrated in the hands of a few, perhaps more now than ever before in history. The poor perennially struggle to regain some of this wealth, often just to survive. Unfortunately, the result of this imbalance is that both the suppressor and the suppressed are forced into disharmony. According to Raimon Panikkar (proponent of interreligious communication and formerly a professor of religious studies at the University of California, Santa Barbara), in a theoretical global village of 100 families before 1990, 90 do not speak English, 65 can't read, 80 have never flown in an airplane, 70 have no drinking water at home, 7 families own 60 percent of the village and consume 80 percent of its energy, and only 1 family has a university education.

In our world today, approximately 40 million people die of starvation each year, according to statistics from the Institute for Food and Development Policy, and approximately 14.5 million of them are children. We have more pounds of ammunition per person than we do of food, according to Doug Mattern, president of the Association of World Citizens. In the 1990s we spent $16,500 per soldier in the world and $260 per child for education. Sources compiled by Greenpeace show that in 1988, in the United States, the richest part of the global village, 1 percent of the population owned 36 percent of the wealth. In 1990 the U.S. ranked last among leading industrialized nations in economic fairness, as defined by the proportion of the income going to the top 20 percent of the population versus that going to the bottom 20 percent. By 2008, the disparity between the rich and poor has gotten even more extreme, with the U.S. still having the greatest disparity. With this huge gap in the distribution of basic resources, we do not have to look far to find the economic causes of war or to understand that starvation is a social disorder. The Essenes taught that this sort of social imbalance comes from disharmony in our personal lives, which then manifests on social and political levels. They felt that both poverty and riches were a result of deviation from the law. The Essenes, although living simply, always had excess food to share with, and personal time for service in, the surrounding communities. One of their great messages that is relevant for our modern world is that if we live by the divine and natural laws we will all experience abundance.

A Peaceful Economy

Economics in the service of peace is part of peace with the community. Our modem economic thinking has some of its roots in the philosophy of Francis Bacon (1561–1626) and Thomas Hobbes (1588–1679), who believed that nature is a limitless resource to be exploited to meet human-ity's personal needs. In their anthropomorphic ego-centered approach, Bacon and Hobbes believed that wealth could be defined as power over other people. In this context, they saw human life as unending competition for power. Adam Smith (1723–1790), in his classic book *The Wealth of Nations,* has often been quoted out of context to support this position of pure *laissez-faire.* Robert Nisbet, who was Albert Schweitzer Professor of Humanities Emeritus at Columbia University in New York, in his book *History of the Idea for Progress,* pointed out that, contrary to the current historical mythology, Adam Smith was deeply sensitive to the needs of the poor and the working class. **Although he was in favor of competition and free enterprise, he always tempered this view with the qualification that people observe the rule of justice.** The current capitalist economists have consistently omitted the rule-of-justice aspect in their citations of Adam Smith to validate their amoral approach to economic thinking. The presence of worldwide hunger, poverty, and economic disharmony in our global village is ample evidence that this approach has not worked for the benefit of humanity or the planet. Clearly, no collective justice has been practiced. The economics of peaceful abundance, which the Essenes successfully demonstrated in their communities, was based on an economic justice for everyone. With global warming becoming a more serious problem, some corporations as well as nations such as Denmark have taken serious steps to shift their economies toward a more environmental conscious perspective.

Yet we still have to ask: Why is there so much poverty, injustice, and environmental degradation on the same planet where there is so much abundance and unparalleled riches? A significant reason is that **our world economic system is not connected to a planetary morality**. As soon as we take economics away from considerations of world peace, prosperity, and service to the whole, and toward the pursuit of personal self-interest, we have sown the breeding grounds of social disorder. Without peace as a consideration in economic decisions, we lack the clarity to make a distinction between useful production and services, such as day-care, afford-able housing, and health care, and those areas of economic productivity that are harmful to humanity, such as the armaments industry, the junk food industry, or the tobacco industry. In 2004, the U.S. military budget was $400 billion, about 40 percent of the worldwide total military spending of $950 billion. It is estimated that an annual expenditure of just $237.5 billion for ten years would provide global health care, eliminate starvation and malnutrition, provide clean water and shelter for everyone, remove land mines, stop deforestation, prevent global warming and acid rain, dissolve the debt of the debtor nations, prevent soil erosion, produce safe and clean energy, and eliminate illiteracy. In other words, we have the ability, with a simple shift in our consciousness and within ten years, to create a world of physical peace. But it must, and does, come from changing our consciousness, which is the source of that shift. To do that we have to face our shadow and let the light guide us to a way of life that leads us to peace. Economics without morality brings chaos and war, not peace. **For economics to aid in the creation of world peace, it must be organized in the service of world peace.**

Conventional economics is presently in conflict not only with social needs, but also with ecological, spiritual, and commonsense needs. In conventional economics, our decisions to exploit natural resources are based on the crudest measure, the price of the commodity on the world market. The more obvious results of this policy are seen in worldwide poverty, in millions of acres of fertile topsoil becoming desert, in global warming, and destruction of the rainforests. In 1987, the World Commission on Environment and Development published a report entitled "Our Common Future." The commission stated:

> Economics and ecology must be completely integrated in decision-making and law-making processes, not just to protect the environment, but also to protect and promote development.
>
> *Greenpeace* magazine, January-February 1989

As economist Herman Daly once said, "There is something fundamentally wrong in treating the earth as if it were a business in liquidation."

Humanity is not in good health; it is being eaten away by the cancer of personal, national, and international separateness and greed. We are still choosing to work only for the ego-centered self, family, or nation. We still seek to take wealth from those we consider outside of us, in whatever way we can. How do we overcome the fear-based greed and the thirst for power and domination that bring so much world disharmony? Through meditation and prayer we are able to go beyond ego-based fear to the direct experience of love and unity. In the condition of harmony, it is fine to seek riches because we are ready to seek them where they really are, in the gold of God Communion. We become so rich in this gold of awareness that we actually want to share our wealth with others. To realize where the real riches are and what they are is the key to creating all levels of personal, familial, national, and international peace.

When enough people experience the golden light of consciousness, international exploitation will be transformed into a new era of economic and social harmony. Then international exploitation will cease on the most fundamental level because we will have learned to keep what is necessary for our material well-being, in a consciousness of abundant simplicity, and to share the rest with our brothers and sisters throughout the world. **Our economics will be in the service of peace.**

The study of our own body function will give us some clues about peace with humanity. How is it that the cells of our body have organized themselves in such a way that they work efficiently and harmoniously with one another to create a healthy body? As the human race, are we so out of control that we cannot do the same? As individuals, we can be likened to the individual cells that make up the human body, just as we make up the planetary human body, and if we could mimic the harmony of our cells as a planetary body, we would all enjoy health, love, and prosperity. In our body, only a cancer cell acts, as we humans do in the world body, separately, disharmoniously, and as a foreigner to the body. The natural and divine laws are played out in the microcosm of our cellular and bodily function as well as in the macrocosm of the world and universe. If we were committed enough to peace to follow these inherent laws on every level of our life, planetary peace would be a real possibility.

The reactivation of the energy of *sacred commerce* and the ancient merchant priesthood is an optimistic answer to the economic imbalances that exist in the world community today. Emerging out of the history of Egyptian teachings of sacred commerce, the pharaoh Akhenaton was said to have passed it on to Moses and the twelve tribes of Israel. (Specific discussions are still found in Jewish literature of the importance of doing business in a way that psychologically uplifts the person one is doing business with, as found in the Torah as well in such current books as *Jewish Ethics and Halakhah for Our Time* by Basil Herring, which covers such merchant priest topics as "the limits of truth and deception in the marketplace.") Merlin and King Arthur's court in the fifth century were associated with sacred commerce, and it was reactivated by the Knights Templar as a way of life and teaching taught by the merchant priesthoods for the creation of peace and the overall uplifting of life on the planet. It can also be found in the teachings of the Prophet Mohammad. We see it worldwide today, such as in the brilliant work of Dr. Mohammad Yunus, who in 1979 founded the first micro-lending bank whose focus was loaning small amounts of money to people (mostly women) in poor rural areas. This concept has spread from Bangladesh to all over the world, and he received a Nobel Peace Prize for this great service. This is just one example of how this understanding is slowly but surely being activated today on this planet.

Sacred commerce is also connected to the rise of the conscious consumer. Best described in the new book *Sacred Commerce* by Ayman Sawaf and Rowan Gabrielle, it is part of overall lifestyle as opposed to a business activity solely for accumulating wealth. It is part of the growing Global Citizen Movement made up of those who choose to live world-healthful lifestyles and interact commercially either consciously or unconsciously using the principles of sacred commerce. It addresses the issues of poverty and war and helps us move from the base of the Maslow pyramid, in which survival and safety are the primary concerns, into a self-actualizing global conscious evolution, a term coined by the visionary Barbara Marx Hubbard. Conscious evolution creates the pre-conditions to act with awareness and intention to create healthy changes in all seven levels of the Sevenfold Path. It creates a conscious ability to address the chaotic conditions of today's temporal reality. The art of the merchant priesthood is to activate and illuminate the divine gift we humans have been given for experiencing the Divine and being peace on the planet. It helps to create a spiritual and intellectual environment that is conducive to democratic principles and freedom; it also helps heal and rebalance the male-female energies to their highest alchemical octave, and enhance the sacred in all aspects of life. It helps one aspect of society from exploiting another aspect of the global community. It creates a healthy water that lifts everyone's boat and the boats of every culture.

In *Sacred Commerce,* the lifestyle practice is defined as the:

> party-cipation of the community in the exchange of information, goods and services that contributes to the revealing of the divine (beauty, goodness, and truth) in all and where spirituality is the bottom line.

In modern times we have known only one bottom line: How much money do I make? As businesses have gotten more sophisticated, that question has multiplied to three bottom-line considerations: What is the intention? What are the means? What is the economic result? Sacred commerce adds a fourth dimension: What is the spiritual return? This becomes the most important bottom-line consideration and simultaneously redefines the meaning of profit. The merchant priests used their business relationships as a feedback system to grow personally and spiritually, especially in the area of character development and as a way to create prosperity and serve humanity. In this context, business is primarily for helping us become more loving, compassionate, caring, happy, and as a way to activate the frequencies of beauty, goodness, and truth. The world of business is a way to create meaning and value, fulfill one's sacred design, and serve the Divine. In this context, the King of Bhutan has created a GNH, or "gross national happiness," as a way to measure the nation's wealth.

These changes represent a global paradigm shift in values and the rise of the global citizenry—people aware of a wider and more interconnected, interdependent world. They are also associated with the 50 million Cultural Creatives in the U.S. who have in common a call for social justice and for a more sustainable, caring world; a world of international cooperation of citizens to make the world a healthier and safer place. They are part of the growing Culture of Life and Liberation that is arising on the planet to see through the misinformation and paranoia on the way to creating a world of peace and fulfillment—a world community filled with peace, prosperity, and conscious evolution for all. The growing merchant priesthood movement is based on people choosing to become agents of goodness and in that context to choose to express their universal love as the desire to work for the good of others. They have become part of the birth of a new humanity.

Respect for International Law

Our institutions reflect our belief systems, and some good progress is being made in the external world, as there is a sense of an increasing shift toward a global awareness. Generally supporting institutions like the United Nations and the World Court, although they are often still embarrassingly sectarian in their decisions, is important because they are the wobbling first steps on a social and political level for creating world peace. The external laws, policies, and efforts at international justice of these institutions support and create an international matrix needed for a shift toward international brother- and sisterhood. Perhaps, as part of this movement toward strengthening international institutions, we are now in the process of a paradigm shift toward respect for civil and human rights as a value system to guide us to work out differences in the world community rather than the old mode of seeing war as a way to solve problems. There will come a time when war will be as outmoded and ethically unacceptable as the institution of slavery.

There is often some public resistance to a shift toward legal, economic, and political cooperation with a larger social unit. The process of expanding our experience of community from smaller social units to larger units, such as in the transition from family to tribe, village to county, county to state, state to nation, and, finally, a planetary shift of individual nations to a global United Nations, encounters the same type of fear and resistance at each step. People fear that expanding their experience of community will weaken their existing unit. Some become afraid that a step toward a higher level of world order will detract from the present family, state, and national unity. What they do not understand is that by creating peace and cooperation with the larger unit, the survival and functioning of the smaller unit is enhanced. There are some very clear problems in creating a one-world government if it is dominated by an oligarchy of wealthy families and corporations, which choose to use the mechanism of a one-world government to further their selfish-egoic desires to exploit resources and peoples, rather than a one-world government created to serve the spiritual health and economic needs of all the peoples of the world. An example of the idea of using the one-world government for personal gain and planetary control is Codex Alimentarius, a World Health Organization idea, which is blatantly controlled by international pharmaceutical companies, the corporate medical-industrial complex in general, and the oligarchy behind them. Their goal is to make herbs, supplements at therapeutic dose levels, and even organic foods illegal while at the same time approving the use of previously banned pesticides and herbicides known to be carcinogens. Codex functionally exists as a means to sacrifice the health of the world for the wealth and world domination of the few. It violates the U.S. Constitution and the right to pursue life, liberty, and the pursuit of happiness. In any commonsense or rigorous examination of the meaning of "life, liberty, and the pursuit of happiness," it is implicit that these rights include the liberty of pursuing and maintaining health.

Restrictive concepts of patriotism are not new to any country and are a force against a one-world government. In the creation of the United States, a similar struggle took place in moving from a loose confederation of thirteen colonies to the formation of a nation. During post-Revolution days, George Washington tried to persuade his New Jersey troops to swear allegiance to the United States. They refused, because they felt that New Jersey was their country. The sentiment against a United States of America was so strong that immediately after the Revolution there was no national government, only the thirteen sovereign colonies. In 1777, representatives of the colonies got together to create the Articles of Confederation and Perpetual Union. After five years, a weak system was ratified that possessed no executive leader, no court system, and no enforceable agreements among the states. Not surprisingly, the Confederation began to fall apart.

Because the Confederation allowed a social chaos that benefited only a few and penalized the vast majority, a constitutional convention was called in 1787. The delegates had to work out a system that neither governed too much, creating another kingship, nor governed too little, allowing anarchy to reign. There was much resistance. It took nine months before the minimum number of nine states needed to bring the U.S. Constitution into existence had signed. Today, it is easy to look back and understand the great benefit of unifying the colonies into the United States on legal, economic, and political levels. On an international level, we are now at a juncture similar to the chaos the colonies faced in 1787. It is now time to expand the vision of peace to include the whole planet.

This transition toward a planetary government is critical if we are to have peace on this planet. Presently, data compiled by Friends of the Earth in the United Kingdom from official sources indicate that an international anarchy allows an ecological pollution of 250,000 tons of sulfuric acid to

CREATING PEACE BY BEING PEACE

fall as acid rain in the northern hemisphere each day, contaminating our water and destroying forests. Each minute, 12,000 tons of carbon dioxide enter the atmosphere, amplifying the greenhouse effect brought about by destruction of the rainforests. Each hour, approximately 1,800 children die of malnutrition, 1,613 acres of productive dryland become desert, 120 million dollars are wasted in global military expenditures. Ten tons of nuclear waste per day are generated by the 360 nuclear plants in the world. Each one is a potential Chernobyl waiting to contaminate the world with radioactive fallout. Perpetual warfare wastes our planetary resources and prevents us from attaining prosperity for every member of the global family and not just for 7 percent of the global family. The cost for the Iraq and Afghanistan wars, as of November 2007, reached beyond $20,000 for a U.S. family of four. The waste and death boggle the mind. This international chaos has created an international paranoia. This is not a peaceful way to live. It disrupts the peace and security of a safe family base. Our children grow up under the threat of instant annihilation. **Without the stabilizing security of planetary peace, every unit of our social system is weakened and disrupted.**

When we talk about peace with community, we have to talk about replacing the law of force with the force of *just* law. The author believes we are about to make the shift to a worldwide acceptance of civil, health, and all levels of basic human rights as the internationally accepted standard of morality. This general acceptance of civil and human rights as a value will eventually be established in our consciousness. Just as the United States had to end the violence of the "Wild West" by bringing law and order to the western states, so we must bring a level of order to the world to end the terror and potential world destruction of the "international Wild West" we have created. Unfortunately, the U.S., along with other major countries, has not been the best example of respecting human rights. This needs to change soon, as worldwide contamination from the use of weapons of mass destruction, such as the use of depleted uranium in armaments, rockets, and bombs in Bosnia, Afghanistan, and Iraq, has had a significant toxic effect on the local and world population. For example, Italian peace observers in Bosnia suffered a rate of leukemia that was three times higher than normal. The statistics from the first Gulf War in Iraq showed increased rates of cancer up to 1,000 percent higher five years later and rates of severe congenital defects up by at least 600 percent. The radiation in some areas of Iraq is 1,000 percent greater than before the first Gulf War. Depleted uranium in this context is a weapon of mass destruction. It is now possessed by seventeen countries. The author and some international lawyers consider this a flagrant disregard of international law based on world treaties dating back to after World War I. If the world national powers feel they are above the law, how can any nation be expected to respect international law? Attempting to solve our international problems by threats and wars of mass murder is simply too primitive.

There are four levels of government in the United States today: city, county, state, and national. One more, an international level of government that truly represents the needs of all the people from a world peace perspective and not simply a lobby for the advancement of national and international corporate agendas, will complete the structure to provide a practical base from which planetary peace has a chance to grow. The establishment of a respected international law gives time for the quality of inner peace to develop. This inner peace is necessary for lasting and fundamental planetary peace. This is like putting a fence around a small tree so that the deer do not eat it. Past U.S. president Harry Truman said:

> When Kansas and Colorado have a quarrel over water in the Arkansas River, they don't call out the National Guard and go to war over it. They bring suit in the Supreme Court of the United States and abide by the decision. There isn't a sane reason in the world why we cannot do that internationally.... It will be just as easy for nations to get along in a republic of the world as it is for you to get along in the republic of the United States.

An international change in attitude by the powerful nations is needed before we can establish any serious international order. This change in attitude will require a change in world consciousness to one dominated by the Culture of Life and Liberation, with love. The power of feeling-based prayer of peace, love, and compassion and the power of meditation are the seed energy to shift world consciousness toward respect for international law and cooperation. Then we will see President Truman's statement be true on an international level. A key attitude behind the success of the constitutional convention of 1787 was the delegates' commitment to acknowledging and reaching agreement about the diversity of needs, lifestyles, and demographics of the different states they represented. This special willingness to compromise is what made peace possible. As Benjamin Franklin delicately put it:

> I confess that there are several parts of this constitution which I do not at present approve. . . . But I am not sure I shall never approve them. For having lived long, I have experienced many instances of being obliged by better information or fuller consideration, to change opinions even on important subjects, which I once thought were right, but found to be otherwise. It is therefore that the older I grow, the more apt I am to doubt my own judgment, and to pay more respect to the judgment of others.

Peace with humanity means a peace in which all nations, all peoples, and all cultures are recognized and respected as an essential part of humanity. It requires compromise in creating a world order that will treat all justly. To achieve peace with humanity, we need to create the conditions for economic, social, political, and spiritual balance in the world. This peace will lovingly end the historical struggle between the haves and have-nots of this world. Peace with humanity will create the preconditions for a stable abundance and tranquility for all.

CHAPTER 6

PEACE WITH CULTURE

Blessed is the Child of Light
Who doth study the Book of the Law
For he shall be as a candle
In the darkness of night,
And an island of truth
In a sea of falsehood. . . .
The written Law
Is the instrument by which
The unwritten Law is understood.

Essene Gospel of Peace, Book 2

Truly, by studying the teachings of ageless wisdom
Do we come to know God,
For I tell you truly,
The Great Ones saw God face to face;
Even so,
When we read the Holy Scrolls
Do we touch the feet of God.

Essene Gospel of Peace, Book 4

PEACE WITH CULTURE INVOLVES HONORING THE ANCIENT
AND PRESENT WISDOM OF ALL CULTURES. Through culture, we
absorb the great teachings that have been given to us by the spiritual masters of all traditions over thousands of years. The Essenes were aware of
three approaches to spiritual evolution: the intuitive path of the mystic,

the path of studying nature, and the path of studying the works of the great masters through their literature and art. They practiced a combination of all three. They studied the great religious works and the works of the great masters. They applied their intuitive and mystical sense, developed by fasting, prayer, and meditation, to intuiting the consciousness of the great masters. This approach allowed them to comprehend the teachings of ancient culture on a deeper level. The Essenes' evolution was also profoundly enhanced by their understanding of the laws of nature. It was customary for everyone to spend a substantial amount of time in the garden. The Essenes were expert in working with trees, plants, and herbs. Mother Nature was one of their greatest teachers.

The core teachings, which exist in all cultures, are important for humanity because they represent the highest ideals from all cultures throughout history. They allows us to connect with the universality of all approaches brought to this planet by the various masters. Those who are unbiased and not threatened by outward differences can see that, at the core level, all teachings reflect the same ageless wisdom. Knowing this ageless wisdom allows us to tap into the evolution of humanity and gives us the perspective that frees us from having to reinvent the wheel or be trapped in separation through focusing on superficial differences. An interesting example of this is M. R. Bawa Muhaiyaddeen, a Muslim teacher who left his body in 1986. His teaching sheds light on the level of misunderstanding of the Koran that the terrorists are promoting to justify their violent Culture of Death:

> In this present century, man has discarded God, truth, peacefulness, conscience, honesty, justice, and compassion. Man has changed so much! Instead of searching to discover the three thousand gracious qualities of God, he has lost all those qualities and opened the way to destruction.
>
> He seeks to ruin the lives of others and to destroy the entire world. With the wealth of God's grace and with the help of His messengers, we must wage a holy war against every one of the four hundred tril-

lion, ten thousand evil qualities that come to destroy our good qualities. This holy war, this jihad, is not something that can be fought on
the outside; our real enemies have been within us from birth. If we
are true human beings *[insan]*, we will realize that. Our own evil qualities are killing us. They are the enemies that must be conquered.

Bawa Muhaiyaddeen

As we rediscover these ancient teachings, we gain support for our own
intuitive insights and spiritual unfolding as well as experiencing the unity
of all cultures. Today, much confusion exists in the rapidly expanding
field of consciousness as well as in the worldwide fundamentalist movements of all religions, because people's understandings and teachings are
not rooted in the soil of ten thousand years of universal spiritual teachings. We would do well to think several times before embarking on a spiritual path that is out of harmony with the ageless wisdom, universal
morality, and universal teachings of all cultures.

The main purpose for studying culture is not to add more factual
knowledge, but to open up to sources of universal wisdom, compassion,
and understanding of all the cultures of the world. We can make contact
with the eternal thinking body of a great master of a culture and thus
imbibe his or her understanding. The great works of art of a Leonardo
da Vinci or a Michelangelo or the music of a Bach, a Mozart, or a Beethoven
reflect the truth of our own Self, the Self of all. The great works of a culture are reflections of the God within all of us, and help us honor and
connect to peoples of all cultures.

On another level, making peace with our own particular background
or culture connects us with our roots. Acknowledging and accepting our
personal roots brings us to a deeper experience of being at peace with
ourselves. Knowing and being at peace with our cultural roots affirms
our connection with historical humanity and helps us to experience ourselves as part of the planetary organism. African Americans in the United
States have placed much emphasis on knowing their roots for this reason.
Native American spiritual teachers have also placed much emphasis on

the remembrance of traditional ways of living. We also sometimes see people who have left the Judeo-Christian tradition to explore other spiritual paths return and attempt to integrate their tradition of birth into the spiritual path that has unfolded for them. For example, about 40,000 post-army service Israeli people per year take a pilgrimage to India. Many of them, as a result of this process, reconnect with their own cultural and spiritual traditions even while in India. Sometimes the experience of another culture helps us reconnect with our own culture of birth.

Peace with culture is also a reflection of how we interact with each other within our own immediate culture. If a national culture suppresses the rights of others to be at peace, the peace of the body, mind, and family of everyone will eventually be disturbed.

MUSIC AS AN EXPRESSION OF PEACE WITH CULTURE

One of the most universal and powerful forms of cultural expression is music. **Sharing music as a cultural gift can serve to melt the ego barriers that separate cultures.**

For example, musicians from cultures throughout the Middle East, including Israel, met in Turkey for a musical gathering. Turkey is one of the few nations where everyone could gather for a mutual celebration of the beauty of life without much difficulty. Sharing music may be one of the most powerful ways of creating a feeling of peace and cooperation among the nations, as people are able to dance to the same beat and experience their basic human unity.

Another example of cultural healing and peace is the three-week Oud Festival in Israel. The oud is the father of the lute, grandfather of the guitar, and considered to be the "sultan" of Arabic musical instruments. The recent 8th International Oud Festival, which included classical Arab, Israeli, and exotic Turkish, Armenian, Bedouin, Sufi, and Middle Eastern liturgical music, was attended by Arabs and Jews of all ages. The explicit goal of the festival was to reactivate the spirit of the Golden Age in medieval Spain, when Jews and Arabs had much in common, shared music, poetry, and art, and lived in peace and harmony. This is the power of peace with culture to create peace. Another example of this, the Festival of Cultural Peace, was held in Jerusalem, Tel Aviv, Petah Tikva, Nazareth, Acre, and Sakhnin.

The Essenes understood how tapping into the power of music to heal the body, strengthen the mind, and unlock the creative spirit could have a transformative effect on both self and society through the vibratory sound current. Music has the power to stir emotions, affect perceptions, and generate a behavioral response pattern. The indisputable fact about music is its power to evoke emotions. The Essenes, according to Dr. Szekely, were very aware about the type of music being created as it knowingly affected community consciousness. Is there anyone for whom music is emotionally neutral?

The power of music to remind the soul of its divine attunement is additionally discovered from spaces opposite of the calm of meditation, such as high-energy mystical trance. In many cultures, it is *normal* for the dancer to be *taken* through the power of music, reconnecting to source energy, reconnecting with ancestors, to touch and bathe the realized Self experiencing the Creator, allowing the dancer to release what does not serve him or her (such as the illusions of fear and pain). Mystical trances through *gnawa* or *qawwalli* music, or through TranceDance rituals, allow willing participants to completely immerse in a practice that has been in many cultures over centuries, with music leading the individuals to sweat their prayers, receive vision, and burn away what does not serve. As early as the cosmic meditation upon AUM (or OM), mystical trances have been in many cultures since the beginning of time. These are alternative sides of the same story, different practices to attain similar results.

Many great classical music composers like Bach wrote at the head of their compositions "A.M.D.G.," the Latin initials for "To the Greater Glory of God." Similarly, when musicians create and perform from a devotional and self-realized state, this intent, at the level of quantum physics, formats their music into an energetic formula that expresses the enlightened perspective of love, or what Pythagoras called "music of the spheres." A series of frequencies and harmonics results that would be analogous to what Abraham Maslow would have described as a state of self-actualization that can bring about thoughts of love, compassion, forgiveness, empathy, and so on—all of the higher orders of thinking that move us from the linear and dualistic view of the world (right/wrong, good/bad, connected/separate) toward a holographic understanding of the divine interconnectedness of all things. The Essenes believed that the soul already operates on the frequency of the "music of the spheres." When we experience sacred music that reflects this harmonic physiologically through the ears and intuitively through the psyche, it is like two computers talking the same protocol; the Law of Sympathetic Vibration dictates that the mind will resonate correspondingly. Therefore, the process of listening to spiritually inspired or sacred music quiets the mind and relaxes the body. In this state, the mind is moved into the presence where the sacred vibration of harmony is least distorted and the mind is quiet enough to both witness and remember the song of the self. Here, the mind is moved from passive hearing to an active listening of the "word" or "primary harmony." In other words, the acts of listening, chanting, or playing sacred music empowers the soul to perceive and release illusions of fear, pain, separation, and suffering so that it experiences and remembers the reality of the love it already is.

> People say that the soul, on hearing the song of creation, entered the body, but in reality the soul itself was the song.
>
> **Fourteenth-century Sufi poet Hafiz**

Research has shown that music has the power to change emotional states, shift our mental outlook, change our physiology, and affect spiritual awareness. Music also has the power to transform individual and collective consciousness into heightened states of love, forgiveness, compassion, and physical healing. These heightened states are also what empowers human awareness to identify societal, geopolitical, and environmental problems and at the same time create and implement solutions for them. This chapter explores the possibility of how creating a culture of peace through spiritually inspired music can shift the collective consciousness so that each of us experiences our innate divinity, and witnesses and recognizes this same divinity in others so that we can recognize the sacredness of our planet's wildlife and natural resources, along with our custodial responsibility for the earth, so that we grow to honor the spiritual, cultural, and ethnic diversity that is the gift of God's creative expression.

> I believe that from the earth emerges a musical poetry which is by the nature of its sources tonal. I believe that these sources cause to exist a phonology of music, which evolves from the universal known as the harmonic series. And that there is an equally universal musical syntax, which can be codified and structured in terms of symmetry and repetition.
>
> **Leonard Bernstein**

The earth and universe, according to all major religious texts, were created and brought into form through sound. The *Bhagavad Gita,* which literally translated means "Celestial Song," states:

> In the beginning was Brahman, with whom was the Word, and the Word was Brahman and Brahman said this world shall be and the world came into being.

Egyptian religious texts state that the singing Sun created the world with its cry of light. The Sun sang: "This world shall be," and the world came into being. From Genesis: "And God said 'Let there be light.'" Similarly, the Gospel of John states: "In the beginning was the Word, and the Word was with God, and the Word was God." And: "The Word was made flesh, and dwelt among us, full of grace and truth." According to John the

Evangelist in the first century AD, the Biblical "Word" can be translated as "Primary Harmony." The religious texts of the Aztecs also referred to God as the "Creator," singing the world into existence. Hindu teachings describe the "Word" in terms of the sound OM, which is the vibratory essence of God and the creative energy used to bring the universe into existence. Buddhists refer to this energy as the primal vibration, teaching that it was divided into twelve tonal derivations, each of which gave rise to and corresponded with the twelve signs of the Zodiac, the twelve months of the year, the twelve hours of the day *(yang)*, the twelve hours of night *(yin)*, and the twelve notes of the chromatic scale.

> All things are aggregations of atoms that dance and by their movement produce sound. When the rhythm of the dance changes, the sound it produces also changes. ... Each atom perpetually sings its song, and the sound at every moment creates dense subtle forms.
>
> **Alexandra David-Néel**

Music and all audible sound, according to spiritual texts, represented the audible manifestation of the "Word," OM, or primal vibration. The great Sufi master Hazrat Inayat Khan went so far as to say:

> What makes us feel drawn to music is that our whole being is music; our mind and body, the nature in which we live, the nature which has made us, all that is beneath and around us, it is all music.

In physics, Einstein's statement that "energy and mass (matter) are different forms of the same thing" creates the foundation for understanding the energetic-vibratory nature of all matter. As energy increases, matter begins to take form. In the nineteenth-century physicist Ernst Chladni (1756–1827, called the "father of acoustics") discovered that when he sprinkled sand onto a flat surface affixed to a pedestal base, and then drew a violin bow perpendicularly across the edge of the surface, round mandala-like shapes were formed as the grains of sand were moved by the sound waves generated. This work was followed by Dr. Hans Jenny

(1904–1972) in a field he named "cymatics," or the study of waves. Jenny was able to capture on a device called a Tonescope the patterns of a circle when OM, the sound associated with creation, was chanted into this device. He also discovered that concentric diamond shapes formed within the circle during the process.

Architecture is crystallized music.

Goethe

Music differs from other art forms such as paintings, sculpture, photography, or literature in that they express more of a linear or one- and two-dimensional form of matter-energy than does music. As such, these art forms are processed by either one or the other brain hemispheres. Music, as a type of matter, remains in a vibratory state and is thus processed holographically, or by both the right (intuitive) and left (analytical) hemispheres of the brain. The philosopher and poet William Kindler proclaimed, "Of all of the arts music is the perfect art, because it strikes the soul without the aid of the intellect." **Creating peace through music is about the use of music as a sympathetic vibration of peace in the heart and soul.**

The Science of the future will be based on sympathetic vibrations.

Rudolph Steiner

Music affects consciousness because of two laws of physics. The first is called the Law of Sympathetic Vibration and the second is the Law of Entrainment. The Law of Sympathetic Vibration works like this: Take two acoustical (string-type) musical instruments such as a piano, violin, or guitar and place them near one another. As the string on instrument A is struck, the vibration from that instrument will resonate and carry across the room, striking the strings on the untouched instrument B and causing it to vibrate. Likewise, this law of physics describes the communication and transference of a song's emotional message (harmony or melody) *from* the mind of the composer and its performers *to* the mind of the listener, thus causing the person to feel and take on the corresponding emotional essence of a song's compositional intent (happy or depressed, peaceful or violent, hopeful or hopeless, and so on). Similarly, the Law of Sympathetic Vibration explains why a person gets goose bumps when listening to a song.

> The companions of right reason are decency, accord, and cadence; decency in song, accord in harmony, and cadence in rhythm.
>
> **Plato**

The Law of Entrainment, or as it is technically called, "mutual phase locking of two oscillators," was first described by a Danish physicist in 1767. This law of physics was discovered one afternoon as the physicist observed the armature motion of two pendulum-type clocks he had placed side by side on a fireplace mantel. In other words, objects (clock armatures) moving in unison (harmony-entrain) express an efficient use of energy. Similarly, the Law of Entrainment is what causes the unconscious neurological tendency of people to move their body or tap their foot in rhythm to music.

> A great musical performance is actually an exercise in the accurate and exquisite communication of emotions. For the audience to feel the emotion in a musical phrase the performer must also feel it in mind, body, and spirit.
>
> **Felix Mendelssohn**

> The noble-minded man's music is mild and delicate, keeps a uniform mood, enlivens and moves. Such a man does not harbor pain or mourn in his heart; violent and daring movements are foreign to him.
>
> **Confucius**

Ancient Chinese philosophers believed that music was an energy formula that could be used for either the benefit of humankind or misused according to free will. One of their most revered texts, *The Spring and Autumn of Lu Bu Ve,* states:

When desires and emotions do not follow false paths, then music can be perfected. Perfected music has its cause. It arises out of justice. Justice arises from the true purpose of the world.

So strong was the Chinese belief in using music to promote peace that every word for music *(yuo)* is represented by the same graphic symbol as the word for serenity *(lo)*. To the Chinese, music represented the highest form of prayer and the most powerful means of directing consciousness toward spiritual realization. Therefore, it was important that composers and performers understand, integrate, and align themselves with the higher-order thoughts of love so that their music promoted a harmonious vision for people.

David Tame, author of *The Secret Power of Music,* states:

Surely the lowest common denominator which determines the precise nature of any musical work is the mental and emotional state of the composer and/or performer. It is the essence of this state which enters into us, tending to mold and shape our own consciousness into conformity with itself. The fact is that all types of musicians, good and bad, tend to be quite aware of the communicative power of tonal art. Through this communicative power, the emotional state of one artist can be transferred to a hundred, or even ten million listeners.

And more, from composers:

The profound meaning of music and its essential aim ... is to produce a communion, a union of man with his fellow man and with the Supreme Being.

Igor Stravinsky

A great musical performance is actually an exercise in the accurate and exquisite communication of emotions. For the audience to feel the emotion in a musical phrase the performer must also feel it in mind, body, and spirit.

Felix Mendelssohn

The relationship between a musician's creative intention and the resulting composition's effect on the emotional and spiritual state of the listener has been a subject of interest for scholars through history. One of the earliest recorded observations was made by Iamblichus, a pupil of Pythagoras:

> And there are certain melodies devised as remedies against the passions of the soul, and also against despondency and lamentation, which Pythagoras invented as things that afford the greatest assistance in these maladies. And again, he employed other melodies against rage and anger, and against every aberration of the soul.

In *Timaeus,* Plato stated:

> Man's music is seen as a means of restoring the souls, rendered confused and discordant by bodily affliction, the harmonic proportions that it shares with the world soul of the cosmos.

Aristotle also concluded:

> Emotions of any kind are produced by melody and rhythm; therefore by music a man becomes accustomed to feeling the right emotions; music has thus the power to form character, and the various kinds of music based on the various modes, may be distinguished by their effects on character—one, for example working in the direction of melancholy, another of effeminacy; one encouraging abandonment, another self-control, another enthusiasm, and so on throughout the series.

From Leo Tolstoy:

> Music is the shorthand of emotions.

And again, from Confucius:

> The superior man tries to promote music as a means to the perfection of human culture. When such music prevails and when people's

minds are lead to the right ideals and aspirations we may see the appearance of a great nation.

Pythagoras, the father of mathematics, believed that the philosophical principles of love, peace, wisdom, compassion, forgiveness, and joy were embodied in the harmonics of what he termed "music of the spheres." This music, as Ancient Greek mystics believed, was heard and recreated in proportion to the composer's level of spiritual evolution and, most important, their intent to create compositions from that devotional mindset. This state of spiritual intention, according to history's great mystics, is accessed through a devotional and contemplative listening to the still small voice within that guides the self into union with Divine Will. "Be still and know that I am God," says the Bible. Paramahansa Yogananda, in *Autobiography of a Yogi,* stated: "The Vedas, India's most ancient scriptures, [were] divinely revealed to the Rishis, or 'seers.' It was a revelation by sound, directly heard." The use of healing music called *ragas* is part of the Indian culture.

> After silence, that which comes nearest to expressing the inexpressible is music.
>
> **Aldous Huxley**

> My soul counseled me and charged me to listen for voices that rise neither from the tongue nor the throat. Before that day I heard but dully, and naught save clamor and loud cries came to my ears; but now I have learned to listen to silence, to hear its choirs singing the song of ages, chanting the hymns of space, and disclosing the secrets of eternity
>
> **Kahlil Gibran**

> From the deeply laid principles of inherited associations, musical tones would be likely to excite in us, in an … indefinite manner, the strong emotions of a long-past age.
>
> **Charles Darwin**

From birth our consciousness is hard-wired to hear and listen. The first bone to develop in the human fetus is the ear bone. The cochlea, part of the inner ear, looks like the shell of a snail. In it are some 60,000 hair cells, each of which resonates like a microscopic tuning fork, to a specific frequency or sound. As one of these hair cells resonates, a corresponding neurological impulse is sent to the brain causing the release of neuropeptides, or "communicator molecules."

> Music is the mediator between the life of the senses and the life of spirit.
>
> **Ludwig van Beethoven**

> Every sickness is a musical problem; the healing therefore, is a musical resolution.
>
> **Novalis, eighteenth-century German mystic and poet**

The healing system of the great Hasidic teacher Rebbe Nachman of Breslov taught that illness occurs when we have lost our holy rhythm. Helping people heal is to find or reactivate their holy rhythm.

In 1964 the renowned biochemist Christian B. Anfinsen drew an interesting analogy between music and protein molecules, stating in the second edition of Stryer's textbook on biochemistry:

> It struck me recently, that one should really consider the sequence of a protein molecule about to fold into a precise geometric form, *as a line of melody written in a canon form and so designed by Nature to fold back into itself, creating harmonic chords of interaction consistent with biological function.*

The renowned Japanese geneticist and evolutionary biologist Susumu Ohno converted the mathematical formulas of living cells into musical notes in an attempt to make the patterns of complex genetic codes more discernible. In an experiment, Ohno reversed the process by converting phosphoroglycerine kinase, an enzyme that enables humans to metabolize sugar, into a mathematical formula and then played its musical equivalent to a group of Japanese kindergartners. He found that it always put the children to sleep because "it sounds like a lullaby." In another he reversed the process, translating the notes of Chopin's funeral march into a chemical equation and found that the entire passage appeared almost identical to a cancer gene found in humans. Ohno concluded:

> This is not surprising; nature follows certain physical laws, the universe obeys them, as does the process of life. Music follows the same patterns as well.

Researcher Dorothy Redlack performed strictly regulated scientific experiments to measure the effects of different types of music on plant growth. In these experiments, music was piped into atmospherically controlled cabinets that housed seedling plants. Over the course of several weeks each of the cabinets were exposed to different types of music for a period of three hours daily. One was exposed to acid rock, another classical music, and another devotional music. Within ten days plants exposed to acid rock began leaning away from the speakers and after a month died. Plants exposed to classical music leaned toward the speakers and grew at a normal rate. However, plants exposed to devotional music leaned toward, wrapped around the speakers, and grew two inches taller than the plants played classical music.

In Dr. William S. Condon's 1975 article in the *Journal of Autism and Childhood Schizophrenia* entitled "The Multiple Response to Sound in Dysfunctional Children," he wrote:

> Just as our internal rhythms are locked on hold with one another they are also *entrained* with the outside world. Our physical and mental states change in rhythm with the seasonal swing of the earth and the sun, with tides, with the day-night cycles and perhaps the cosmic rhythms that present-day science has yet to isolate and define. *When these rhythms are forced out of phase, disease is likely and dis-ease is inevitable.*

Plato, again, in *Laws:*

> Through foolishness they deceived themselves into thinking that there
> was no right or wrong in music—that it was to be judged good or bad
> by the pleasure it gave. By their work and their theories they infected
> the masses with the presumption to think themselves adequate judges.
> ...As it was, the criterion was not music, but a reputation for promis-
> cuous cleverness and a spirit of law-breaking.

And Confucius, again:

> If one desires to know if a kingdom is well governed, if its morals are
> good or bad, the quality of the music will furnish the answer.

The importance of music for healing and elevating the consciousness
of the people is well understood by musicians. For example, renowned
violinist Isaac Stern asserted:

> Everything we do is connected to music. Civilization is based on a
> certain level of discipline and order, and this is the essence of the struc-
> ture of music.

There is a relationship between the music children listen to and the
way they might act and grow up. An article in *ADWEEK* noted that
"teenagers and young adults buy more albums than their elders and are
more likely to take their message to heart, whether philosophy, politics,
or style." If this is so, consider how Nirvana's 1993 album *In Utero* ("in
the womb"), which sold more than 9 million units worldwide and featured the song written by Kurt Cobain entitled "I Hate Myself and Want
to Die" might have influenced its listeners. Coincidently, in this same year
the American Psychiatric Association's annual report found that "3 to 6
million U.S. children are clinically depressed." In 1994 Pearl Jam sold
almost 4 million units of *Vitalogy,* an album that featured a song that lyri-
cally described a child explaining to a therapist why spankings are better
than hugs "because you get closer to the person." A review by KRT News

said the album's lyrics provided a "harrowing observation that reminds us how effective Pearl Jam has been in using pain to make that valued connection with its fans." In that same year UNICEF's year-end report found that the U.S. ranked third in the world in youth suicides. Henry David Thoreau made it clear that the effect of music on society is powerful when he said:

> Even music can be intoxicating. Such apparent slight causes destroyed Greece and Rome, and will destroy England and America.

In 1993 Dr. Jonathan Klein published results of his survey of 2,760 adolescents ranging from 14 to 16 years of age: "There is clearly an association between embracing heavy metal music and risky behavior (smoking marijuana, cheating, stealing, drinking, alcohol and having sex)." This same year Snoop Dogg released his album *Doggy Style*, which sold almost 1 million units in its first week on sale. Lyrics from the album stated: "Walking down the street smoking indo [marijuana] sipping on gin and juice. . . . Later on that day my boy Dr. Dre came through with a gang of Tanqueray and a fat ass J of some blue bonic chronic [marijuana]." A 1995 University of Michigan study found: "One in four school children have used illegal drugs before reaching high school." This same year Green Day, *Rolling Stone* magazine's Band of the Year, released their album *Dookie*, which sold more than 5 million units. Lead band member Mike Dirnt was quoted in a feature article: "I think drinking and doing drugs are very important. Everybody should drop acid at least once." In this same interview Billie Joe Armstrong, lead guitarist and vocalist for the group, stated: "Say you hate somebody, and you sit and think about every possible way that you could kill them. You're like 'I f**king hate 'em.' . . . That's what I like to write about." Obviously, the consciousness of the musicians affects the energy of their music, which in turn affects the consciousness of the musician's culture, which in turn affects the consciousness of the people and all the other future musicians coming out of the culture. The consciousness of culture creates musicians who reflect and affect the culture.

Our music can either reflect the lowest emanations of a culture such as fear, hate, and murder, or those of peace, compassion, and love. What do we choose to listen to and what does the mass media, which usually reflects the Culture of Death, promote? **As we create a world culture of peace, it is important to create a world music that shares the vibration of peace and love and in the process creates a sharing of the best of the different world cultures, which in turn creates respect for all the gifts of the different planetary world cultures.** The real power of culture through music is the potential to spread the vibration of the joy of inner and outer peace through the subtle effect of music on the heart and mind.

MUSIC IN THE CULTURE OF LIFE AND CULTURE OF DEATH

The Essenes, the Sufis, the Native Americans, the Gnostics, the Hindus, and many other cultures throughout the planet understood how tapping into the power of music could have a transformative effect on both self and society.

As time has progressed, and many cultures have drifted from their nomadic centers into urban dwellings, musical and artistic expressions have moved from the praise and folkloric songs around the fire to singing along with the latest pop radio hit. The ear-candy of the three-minute pop song is the equivalent of a microwave meal, minus the nutritious weight of the soundtrack of days past. Most music today directly infects minds and ears with cavity and decay, influencing and dummifying the general public with mental and spiritual toxins—the radio of our modern culture works toward putting the general public into mental slavery. On a planetary level we witness the idolification of the gangster and the music industry's consumer propaganda and justification that violence and hatred are accepted behaviors. "My mind on my money and my money on my mind" is the deeply embedded mantra of this era. There is no wrong in managing one's financial affairs, yet the values of our consumer-driven society seem to be the only soundtrack heard by the numbed millions of Americans leading lives centered around shopping, credit cards, and a life of debt. This soundtrack advertises the mantra forward, infecting young people with the presumption "me first and money is God" that has spread across the planet like a deadly virus.

> I'm out for presidents to represent me. Get money!
> I'm out for dead f**king presidents to represent me.
>
> Jay-Z

The Culture of Death is a culture of debt, where the mass brainwashing of billions seeking satisfaction in the accumulation of gadgets, the latest styles, expensive cars, and jewelry is constantly propelled forward by greed-based economics through music. The mind- and heart-influencing machine of "receive for self alone" is found in 99 percent of the culture of popularly ingrained music, from hip-hop to pop, shackling and desensitizing global citizens in a common dysfunctionality.

The Culture of Death is a culture advocating violence as normal. Through song and every visual medium, the solution to all conflicts comes with weapon and ammunition. Our planet faces a drought of peaceful solutions seeking reconciliation without bloodshed. Oppression is applauded and rewarded with diamonds, today's hip-hop boy's best friend. A culture that stands for war and invasion is being accompanied by a soundtrack that promotes the gangster of drugs and killing. What do we stand for in such a culture? In this climate, what of this culture are we wearing? Empowerment with a gun in our hand is the song of the day. "Dollar Dollar Bills" is the song of the day. Has this mind-numbing soundtrack taken the real fight out of listeners? As John Lennon so simply stated: "Give Peace a Chance."

The Culture of Life and Liberation is peace supported through blessing, seeing the beauty in others, compassion, faith, and reconciliation— the space where all sides might not be able to agree, but can express truthfully, sincerely, and agree to disagree. Sing me a solution for the challenges providing options, giving life, support, and a helping hand. The Culture of Death is preying upon ignorant minds, praying upon false idols, especially the highest almighty, the dollar. The Culture of Death is a culture of violence, expressing intolerance exercised behind the smoke of a gun and the impact of a police baton.

> If you get down and quarrel every day, you're saying prayers to the devil, I say.
>
> Bob Marley's "Positive Vibration"

Planetary airwaves are polluted with toxic music promoted by corporate and governmental interests. A decontamination of the arts is needed for institutions such as Clear Channel and Viacom. There is the story of ratings and feeding the public what it responds to—sex and violence sell, as in the decadent age of gladiators in ancient Rome, where internal decay resulted in the collapse of a once mighty civilization. Another civilization fueled by greed and blood and the numbing of the minds of its populace is our own. The shadow of the Culture of Death runs far and long in U.S. history, where we have seen a continuous cycle of an-eye-for-an-eye rationalizations—injustice met with injustice, violence met with violence, greed met with greed, revenge met with revenge. Give peace a chance.

Mythic tales of the Age of Aquarius igniting the emotions of a growing movement of "enlightened beings" point toward the hope of planetary evolution. Yoga centers in America are as common as cafes in France. For the first time in history the planet has access not only to the same pop culture, but also to the rich wisdom traditions and musics of the world. Beacons of light shine in the great blinding shadow of the Culture of Death. Exposure to different cultures and the growing market for "world music" further expands the Culture of Life and Liberation, including nations and traditions beyond American borders. Are we not a nation of immigrants? The future voices of American are not only black and white, but Indian, Arab, Hispanic, Asian, and African, taking old ideas from their homelands and adopting them in new and innovative ways, furthering not only the acceptance of different cultures, but inviting the global citizen. The Culture of Life and Liberation is a movement of welcoming, beyond just tolerance.

> I can change the world, with my own two hands, make it a better place, with my own two hands, make it a kinder place, with my own two hands, with my own, with my own two hands.
>
> Ben Harper's "With My Two Hands"

Slowly, the Culture of Life and Liberation is spreading. You will not find the signs on TV and radio—look elsewhere. Although in small increments, the Culture of Life and Liberation is growing. On a musical level, we have inspiring melody and rhythm that can stir the soul, inspire ecstatic dances of liberation, and trigger gratitude. Pop groups such as Inner Voice are singing about Buddha and Krishna and chanting "I Am Holy" in their song "Holy." Ziggy Marley is carrying the torch of his father, proclaiming: Love is my religion, Love is my religion, Love is my religion. Hey, you can take it or leave it, and you don't have to believe it." Without any airplay or popular support, devotional artist Krishna Das sells tickets to thousands, singing "I have found a way to live in the presence of the Lord, Hare Ram Ram Ram." Pop icon Sting directs radio listeners to "Send your love into the future."

> What's so funny about peace, love, and understanding?
>
> Elvis Costello

> *Emancipate yourselves from mental slavery;*
> *None but ourselves can free our mind.*
> *Have no fear for atomic energy,*
> *'Cause none of them-a can-a stop-a the time.*
> *How long shall they kill our prophets,*
> *While we stand aside and look?*
> *Yes, some say it's just a part of it:*
> *We've got to fulfill de book.*

Won't you help to sing
These songs of freedom?
'Cause all I ever had:
Redemption songs
All I ever had:
Redemption songs.
These songs of freedom
Songs of freedom.

Bob Marley

We are all evolving; it is happening slowly or too fast, depending on one's reference. The Culture of Life and Liberation can only grow, as it is our human instinct and drive to respond and transcend the Culture of Death. As the Rastafarians so eloquently stated, we must "Chant Down Babylon." For example, the most popular Israeli band, Sheva, has inspired thousands with the musical lyrics of peace, love, and God that help us break the shackles of the Culture of Death. **In an era of great upheavals and global emergency, there is a new global emergence of the power of the Culture of Life and Liberation music, which inspires people to live at the highest octave of peace, love, and the Divine. This new music helps create an intercultural resonance beat, which dissolves the walls between the different world cultures, and strengthens the Culture of Life and Liberation in all.**

ACKNOWLEDGING THE RIGHT OF THE OTHER CULTURE TO EXIST

What seems to be the key to make one joint Arab and Jewish Israeli community work is that each culture affirms the right of the other to exist while living in cooperation with each other. The key principle for establishing and maintaining peace is affirming the right of the other culture to exist. This, of course, is an obvious model for creating peace in the Middle East as well as in the world. Allowing the expression of joy and peace creates peace within the culture. Peace with culture means allowing the full expression of peace in culture to evolve, and being in harmony with this expression. It means allowing our culture to reflect the eternal truth in us. Although not perfect, Iran was a model in which the Jewish culture was allowed to peacefully exist for 2,500 years. Members of the remaining community of 25,000 Jews in Iran, in 2008, still insist they are well treated and their existence is respected. Jewish people who have migrated from Iran do not necessarily support this position. In Morocco, also a Muslim state, the Jewish culture still peacefully exists. In Israel, Muslim and Christian Arabs and Christians of both Eastern and Western traditions, different nomadic cultures, atheists, and a variety of Jewish subreligions and subcultures exist in relative respect and safety, compared to the rest of the world. Even in the most difficult circumstances, such as in the Middle East, peace with culture is possible.

This simple, fundamental, and obvious approach to peace, acknowledging the right of the other to exist, works. The rest is working out the details. The author appreciates the clear statement of Hamas and Hezbollah in 2008 (when this book was published)—that they do not acknowledge the right of Israel to exist. This honest statement by these organizations lets everyone know where they stand and allows for clear choices that need to be made if peace in the Middle East is to happen. Family therapists know that there cannot be healing in a family system if people are not honest with each other. Peace with culture is the ability to move beyond ego and ethnocentric views of the world to a world-centric view in which we acknowledge our oneness and agree on the right of the other to exist. Any so-called peace agreement without this fundamental sincere commitment and acknowledgment of the right of the other to exist is unlikely to succeed.

This brings us to a most difficult issue in an authentic peace discussion. The question is classically symbolized by English Prime Minister Neville Chamberlain's failed "appeasement strategy," offering Hitler one country at a time in Europe. It failed because Chamberlain did not recognize Hitler's presumption that no culture but the Third Reich had a right to exist, and his intention to make it so. Hitler, as a self-confessed pagan, believed in the survival of the fittest, which meant that, in his view, he had a right to dominate the world and eliminate all cultures that threatened his world-view. At some point, the world powers realized they had no alternative but war to defeat him.

As with family therapy, there is not always a single right answer to the question of when one makes a choice for divorce. It is the same when cultures or countries understand that because another culture or country does not agree on the right to exist that they are left no alternative but war. In the twentieth century, we saw the Armenian genocide and the Holocaust, along with genocides in Darfur, Bosnia, and Rwanda. They remind us that at some point, when someone believes you have no right to exist, you need to choose to fight back—a peaceful solution no longer is an alternative.

One of Gabriel's spiritual teachers, Swami Prakashananda, knew Gandhi and marched with him; he was even wounded by gunshot during their nonviolent crusade. In a private communication to the author, Swami Prakashananda pointed out, along with several other Indian spiritual people who marched with Gandhi, that for Gandhi the nonviolent strategy, although a strong part of his spiritual teaching, was also based on a belief that the British government had a certain morality and did believe that Indians had a right to exist. This was also true for the strategy of the civil rights movement in the United States led by Dr. Martin Luther King, Jr., which succeeded because of the deep moral sensitivity in white America that African Americans had the right to exist and the right to civil rights, which is one step further than the right to exist.

It brings us back to the difficulty of when we're really faced with a hard-core belief that those in another culture don't believe you have a right to live. At what point do you realize that peace negotiations are simply manipulations and strategies to gain a more powerful position. These are extremely difficult questions.

It is the role of the peacemakers to create such a strong planetary thought form of peace that everyone's consciousness evolves to the point of realizing that the other has a right to exist. Only then can true peace negotiations actually happen. When this consciousness is present, there will be war no more.

A perfect example of this principle was the Essenes joining with the Maccabees to fight against the Greco-Syrian (Seleucid) Empire of Antiochus Epiphanes, who did not recognize the right of the Jews to exist and had even outlawed Judaism's most basic practices and symbols (including circumcision, Sabbath observation, and possession of the Torah) on pain of death. He had tried to force the priests to make offerings of pigs (unkosher meat) and to eat the offerings. The killing of mothers with their circumcised babies made it clear that he was viciously and violently denying the right of the Jews to exist. With the survival of their culture at stake, the Jews, lead by the Maccabees and joined by the Righteous Ones (the Essene holy warriors known as the Hasidim or the pious ones), began revolts starting in the town of Modi'in 17 miles north of Jerusalem in 167 BCE. Empowered with the joining of these Hasidim, the Maccabees had enough men with military experience to conduct a guerrilla-type warfare against the overwhelming superior numbers of the Seleucids and their Hellenistic Jewish allies. (See 1 Maccabees 2:42.) Oral and written tradition tells us that the Essenes were both skillful and fierce spiritual warriors, forming the backbone of this successful revolution after a three-year struggle. The point of the example is clear: The Essenes lead a nonviolent peaceful life in their communities and with others in the area, but when their right to exist became irrevocably challenged, they adopted a strategy of violent resistance that saved the Jewish existence.

As a son of Avraham, the universalist, being the message of the One God to all cultures, Gabriel is comfortable with all the children of Avraham and their various cultures. There is a growing movement among the children of our essential oneness, and of the heartfelt brotherhood and sisterhood of people in the three religions-cultures as we share the understanding of the Culture of Life and Liberation. However, we are still a minority. Gabriel's Arab Palestinian brothers and sisters are still at physical risk if they speak the truth to the dominant Culture of Death, which does not want peace in the Middle East. For example, Iyad Barghouti, director of the Ramallah Human Rights Center, says the Al-Aqsa TV is a disturbing milestone in the rise of Islamist forces. Dr. Sami Alrabaa, a sociology professor in Germany and a columnist for the *Kuwait Times,* in a 2007 article titled "The Culture of Hatred," strongly criticized the Hamas Al-Aqsa Television for its hate-inspired Mickey Mouse program that encourages and inoculates this culture of hatred and death toward those who are different. He points out that secular and moderate Palestinians are appalled by the extremist propaganda of Hamas TV. Alrabaa describes himself as "one of those who have tried (without success) to publish articles about the Arab-Israeli conflict, telling readers that the image of Israel as presented in the belligerent Arab discourse is distorted and fabricated." The point is that to create a climate that is conducive to peace making, as Alrabaa directly puts it, "The culture of hatred must stop." Unfortunately, these subcultures of hate exist within the Culture of Death all over the world, and this exposure by an insider makes the point clear that any consideration for a serious and lasting peace requires addressing the dissonance of these subcultures of hate.

Conclusion

Why is peace with culture so important? Cultures are the extension of the ego. They are an extension of ways of life and belief systems that reflect thought forms. These thought forms are an expression of the body-mind-I Am ego state. They are not a problem as long as one realizes what they are and does not attempt to inflict them on people of other cultures who do not share the same thought forms. The thought forms of one culture or religion are not necessarily universal truths. These thought-belief systems do not justify destroying another culture, or even one person, and certainly not the living planet. To engage in these destructive intercultural behaviors at this time in history takes us back to the cause of war, which is "the more I have (extension of thought form domination over another culture by force), the more I am." It is, as it always has been, a recipe for war. Music has the ability to take us beyond cultural thought forms to a peaceful place of unity in which we are all dancing to the subtle beat of the Divine.

Shared music of peace, which is emerging in the Middle East, in which all cultures open their hearts through music, is a powerful antidote to the Culture of Death and allows people to experience that we all reflect the rhythm and music of God. The Culture of Life and Liberation, by recognizing that all cultures have the right to exist and all people are lovable sparks of God, sets the preconditions for real peace. With this more evolved consciousness people may create a variety of geographic states, but there will be only one state of consciousness: a single state of love, forgiveness, blessing, and support for the right of all people to exist and to dance the holy rhythm of the Divine in their own way.

CHAPTER 7

PEACE WITH THE
LIVING ECOLOGY

Blessed is the Child of Light
Who knoweth his Earthly Mother,
For she is the giver of life.
For know that thy mother is in thee,
And thou art in her.
None can live long,
Neither be happy,
But he who honors his Earthly Mother.

Essene Gospel of Peace, Book 2

PEACE WITH THE LIVING ECOLOGY IS THE FOUNDATION OF OUR PHYSICAL AND SPIRITUAL EXISTENCE ON THIS PLANET.

Peace with nature requires us to attune ourselves and be sensitive to our inner nature so that we are able to know nature as an extension of our Self. One aspect of this peace is the ability to resensitize ourselves to nature, to feel her energies, to know and cooperate with her laws, and to become one with them as a natural expression of who we are. **Peace with nature involves understanding that we are but one strand in the web of life—we are not the whole web.** Nature is a reflection and a reminder of our Creator. Our love of nature enhances our communion with the Divine.

To be at peace with nature is to accept that, on the physical plane, we are affected by the forces of nature. In understanding this, we discover that vibrant health depends on adequate sunlight, clean air, pure water, and healthful, uncontaminated food. Understanding that the health of our physical bodies depends on maintaining a healthy planet, we get another level of understanding of our mutually dependent interaction with nature. What is good for our bodies is also healthy for the living planet. If we pollute the living planet for our economic and personal egoic needs, it reflects back to us in increased pollution of our physical bodies. According to research monitored by the Environmental Defense Council, the average umbilical blood of a baby born in the U.S. has an average of 200 toxins—up to 217 neurotoxins and 180 carcinogens. It is no wonder that the leading cause of death from disease among children age 15 and younger is cancer. Our reckless and unconscious pollution of the environment is a violation of the living planet and the shared space, which results in the toxic violation and increased rates of death of our own children. The economic and ego-centered violation of the living planet has been acknowledged by almost all people and nations as the cause of global warming. In essence, global warming with its increase of more serious level 5 hurricanes is a symptom of the Culture of Death. Other earth changes, like Type 2 diabetes—which has been declared by the U.N. in late 2007 an international health problem and pandemic, from which 246 million people worldwide suffer—are symptoms of the Culture of Death. An aspect of the worldwide Culture of Death lifestyle is a world-view based on a sense of separation and exploitation of the living planet, as compared to the world-view of the Culture of Life and Liberation, which is based on a sense of oneness and living in harmony with the living planet and all its inhabitants. The differences in the manifestations of these two world-views are becoming more and more obvious.

Every nation of this world is subject to the laws of nature. For example, in the book *Topsoil and Civilization* by Vernon Carter and Tom Dale, a clear link is established between the decline of a civilization and soil erosion destroying its fertility base. Topsoil is nutrient-rich soil that holds moisture and in which our crops grow. It is the basic foundation of our sustenance on this earth. The U.S. Department of Agriculture has acknowledged a drop of 70 percent in cropland productivity as an unparalleled disaster. Two hundred years ago, the U.S. had 21 inches of topsoil; now we have approximately 6 inches left. According to Dr. Szekely, "Universal history shows that every nation reached its greatest splendor by following the great law of unity between man and nature." Dr. Szekely points out that history shows that when a nation led a simple life of cooperation with nature, that nation flourished, but when the nation deviated from this unity, it inevitably disintegrated or disappeared. We are but human organisms living in the topsoil, along with all the other organisms. When the topsoil is destroyed, we are too.

This law of unity between humanity and nature was held by the Essenes to be the guide to how we should live in the material world. The *Zend Avesta,* a collection of Zoroastrian prayers, hymns, and wisdom by Zarathustra, taught that the ideal existence entails always keeping in contact with the forces of nature. This law of unity is the foundation for how we may best organize our life on the planet if we are to have a healthy humanity. **At this point in our planetary history, if we are simply to survive, we need to follow the law of unity between humanity and nature. If we keep trying to break the laws of nature, they will eventually break us.**

Unfortunately, since the beginning of the Industrial Revolution, we seem to have forgotten this law of unity with nature. In the last thirty years alone, we have destroyed more of our planetary environment than in all of the previous cataclysmic events of previous civilizations. We exploit nature rather than act as co-creators with nature. We treat nature as an alien force to be fought and conquered. In 1854, Chief Seattle, in his famous address to the president of the United States, warned us to respect the earth as our mother:

> His appetite will devour the earth and leave behind only a desert. . . . Whatever befalls the earth befalls the sons of the earth. If men spit upon the ground, they spit upon themselves. . . . Contaminate your bed, and you will one night suffocate in your own waste.

Because of our ignorance, greed, and alienation, we are actively disrupting the ecology of this planet. According to statistics compiled by Friends of the Earth in the United Kingdom, each minute 51 acres of tropical forests are destroyed and 50 tons of fertile topsoil are washed or blown off cropland. Every hour approximately 1,600 acres of productive dryland become desert. Famine is now a regular phenomenon as desert land grows. Each day 25,000 people die because of water shortage and water contamination. Each day 60 tons of plastic packaging are dumped into the sea, along with 372 tons of fishing nets discarded by commercial fishermen. One species becomes extinct every five hours. The greenhouse effect is changing our weather.

People are afraid of our friend the sun because of a thinning ozone layer and consequently try to shield themselves from the nourishing sun. Is this an exaggerated problem? Not if you consider that 20 minutes in the sun stimulates up to 20,000 IU of vitamin D, and many experts agree that adequate vitamin D, which is made in the skin as a result of sun exposure, activates the immune system and decreases the incidence of almost all cancers by up to 70 percent. A world culture not in peace with the living planet jeopardizes world civilization as well as personal health in a variety of complex ways that are often beyond our personal understanding. A heartfelt connection with the living planet, based on love and spiritual awareness of our oneness with all of life as part of the living biophoton field, naturally leads us into basic harmony with the living planet and guides our living with the laws of nature.

Contrary to a Culture of Life and Liberation world-view, which honors a healthy spiritual love relationship with the living planet as a normal way to live one's life, our present industrial system, the expression of the Culture of Death, focuses on the accumulation of wealth rather than on peace with nature. Greed leads nations to forget the unity of humanity and nature. One concrete example of this breakdown is the ecological disaster in Poland reported by Sabine Rosenbladt in *Greenpeace* magazine, November-December 1988. In 1985 the Polish parliament recognized four areas of its country as pollution disaster areas, including the Gdansk Bay area, the industrial areas of Upper Silesia, the Krakow area, and the copper basin of Liegnitz-Glogow. By Poland's own industrial standards, these areas were so contaminated with industrial and municipal pollution that the people living there, representing 30 percent of Poland's population, should be evacuated. In the Baltic Sea, seven nations yearly dump 125,000 tons of heavy toxic metals, one million tons of nitrogen, 70,000 tons of phosphorus, and 50,000 tons of oil and highly toxic PCBs. Because of this irresponsibility, Poland's Gdansk Bay, situated on the Baltic Sea, now has 100,000 square kilometers of sea floor declared biologically dead. The fish are almost gone. One local fisherman said that the last eels caught in the bay were so corroded by toxic chemicals that "they looked like they were already cooked." The drinking water of Gdansk was so polluted that one environmentally concerned Polish biophysicist said that the term "drinking water," as a label for what comes out of the tap, is used only for the sake of nostalgia. According to official 1984 Polish statistics, 71 percent of the nation's drinking water was disqualified by the national public health authorities for hygienic reasons. In Krakow, one of the other disaster areas, the life span is three to four years shorter than that of the rest of the population. The rate of cancer in Krakow, especially of lung cancer, is higher than in other areas, as is the rate of allergies, chronic bronchitis, degenerative bone diseases, circulatory illnesses, and infant mortality. In Glogow, another disaster area, contaminated fields continue to be farmed; 20 percent of the food tested from these areas is classified as hazardous to public health. Vegetables were found to have 220 times the acceptable limit for cadmium, 165 times for zinc, 134 times for lead, 34 times for fluorine, and 2.5 times for uranium. Green lettuce grown near Krakow contained 230 milligrams of lead per kilo. These statistics reflect concretely what is meant when humanity and nature are not in harmony. The case of Poland, confirmed back to 1984, points to the worldwide ecological disaster that is currently underway. **To create peace in the world requires that we pay attention to our waste products. As an herbalist** friend of mine once said, "Pay attention to your elimination or it will eliminate you." Peace with the environment requires that we pay attention and do something now.

More countries are beginning to pay attention to the disastrous effects of the pollution on our personal health and planetary health, but the gap is a big one between attention and responding appropriately. At an international conference in Bali in 2007, negotiators from approximately 190 nations tried to discuss an emissions control framework. But environmental damage continues to exceed expectations. For example, a report, cited in *Christian Science Monitor,* December 3, 2007, by the U.S. National Oceanic and Atmospheric Administration, the National Center for Atmospheric Research, and two universities says that the tropical climate belt has widened by 2–4.8 degrees of latitude between 1979 and 2005, and that this is an expansion rate expected only later this century. Scientists have noted that since 2000, global emissions have grown at a rate higher than all but the highest projections posited by the U.N.-sponsored Intergovernmental Panel on Climate Change for global warming. Although the 5 percent emissions cut by 2020 suggested by the 1997 Kyoto Agreement is not nearly enough to reduce global warming, the U.S. is the only country not even ready to ratify this mild approach. The good news is that some countries are responding. China is trying to cut its country's economy's greenhouse-gas intensity by 20 percent between 2005 and 2010. Brazil has pledged to cut its country's rate of deforestation by 50 percent. States like California have taken the initiative to go beyond federal government guidelines. Some European cities such as Stockholm and London have also installed progressive initiatives that go beyond international treaties. Gussing, Austria has cut its emissions by 90 percent. Apeldoorn in the Netherlands is aiming at 100 percent by 2020. Vaxjo, Sweden, has cut emissions by 30 percent and its goal is 50 percent by 2010. The point is that it can be done. Of Europe's core fifteen nations, however, only Britain, France, Germany, and Sweden are looking like they will succeed in meeting Kyoto commitments. Unfortunately, global CO_2 emissions have risen by 2.9 percent per year since 2000, compared to an 0.7 percent rise per year in the 1970s. U.S. emissions have risen 16.3 percent from 1990 to 2005, and China's total emissions of 6.2 billion tons is beyond the 5.8 billion tons of the U.S.

The latest report in 2007 by the Intergovernmental Panel on Climate Change (IPCC) is that in order to hold global warming to about 3.6°F (2°C) by 2100, industrial countries need to reduce greenhouse gas emissions 25–40 percent below 1990 levels by 2020. Environmentalists suggest that a mean global temperature increase of more than 3.2°C greater than pre-industrial levels will be enough to create disastrous consequences of global warming, and anywhere between 3 and 5 degrees C will probably take us to a complete melt of the Greenland ice sheets, a collapse of the Amazon rainforest, and sea-level rise of 10 to 20 meters. Moderation, in terms of global warming and the outcome of the Bali Conference, destroys. Not setting specific emission targets, as decided at this Bali Conference, is not even moderate, but Mother Earth will continue to speak back on the issue by increasing the heat and other earth changes until we as a world are wise enough to respond.

And people of all walks of life are beginning to respond. More than 100 evangelicals, according to the *Christian Post,* have signed the Evangelical Climate Initiative, which concluded that global warming is real and states:

> Christians, noting in fact that most of the climate change problem is human induced, are reminded that when God made humanity he commissioned us to exercise stewardship over the earth and its creatures. . . . Climate change is the latest evidence of our failure to exercise proper stewardship, and constitutes a critical opportunity for us to do better.

Rabbi Julian Sinclair, co-founder of Tikkun ha Olam, the Jewish initiative on climate change, is quoted in the *Jerusalem Post:* "Religion is uniquely able" to mobilize "far-reaching changes in individual behavior." He concludes:

Let us kindle all of our Hanukka candles this year, and see in their light the hope that together we can act to ensure a safe climate future for ourselves, our children, the world's poorest and most vulnerable people, and all the creatures with whom we share God's earth.

The Associated Press reports:

The haves—which pump the lion's share of pollutants into the atmosphere—are arguing about emission targets and high-tech solutions. The have-nots—which contribute little to global warming but are disproportionately among the victims—need tens of billions of dollars to save [them].

At least there are enough conscious people and nations to begin to understand that peace with the ecology is important. Another example in the U.S. of this struggle is the battle over the Clean Water Act, whose thirty-fifth anniversary was in October 2007. It has been a successful law protecting all U.S. waters, but the rather confused Rapanos decision by the U.S. Supreme Court has temporarily undermined the Clean Water Act. The good news here is that a bipartisan group of 170 representatives have created the Clean Water Restoration Act (H.R. 2421). It is being opposed by a coalition of polluting industries, including gas and oil developers, the mining industry, electric utilities, pesticide companies, homebuilders, and the Farm Bureau. Earthjustice and a coalition of national, state, and local environmentalists, as well as the governors of Arizona, New Mexico, Montana, and Wisconsin, along with the attorneys general of California, Connecticut, Delaware, Maine, Maryland, Massachusetts, New Hampshire, New Jersey, New York, Oregon, Rhode Island, the District of Columbia, and Vermont, as well as labor leaders representing the United Steel Workers, American Institute of Architects, and the Pacific Coast Federation of Fishermen Associations all support the bill.

There is a basic Torah principle which all environmental struggles are about:

Thou shalt have a place outside the military camp, whither thou shalt go forth abroad. And thou shalt have a spade among thy weapons; and it shalt be when thou sittest down outside, thou shalt dig therewith, and shalt turn back and cover that which cometh from thee.

Deuteronomy 23:13–15

In other words, we are not allowed to defecate in the public commons, even in the time of war. The air, earth, water, and sun are the commons of all the Earth's inhabitants. Although the issue of polluting the commons was clarified 3,600 years ago, the Culture of Death still values the wealth of the few over the health of the many. **This issue is fundamental for peace with the ecology. It is more than a survival issue; it is an ancient and valid, practical, spiritual principle that one is not allowed to pollute the shared public space, or commons.**

A stronger commitment is needed, but the energy of the Culture of Death makes it hard to let go. Just as with meditation, the more cities and nations commit to radical transformation in their energy approach, the more others will follow. As the survival of the world depends on it, more people, cities, states, and nations will come to their senses and do what is necessary. We will understand that high energy consumption—personal, economic, political, ecological, and spiritual—is not aligned with well-being on every level.

THE GAIA HYPOTHESIS

Interestingly enough, our own technology has provided us with a modern conceptual understanding that may inspire us to reestablish our unity with nature. This insight is called the Gaia hypothesis. NASA has developed an instrument called the telebioscope, which, when placed upon various spacecrafts, can determine if life exists on various planets. One experiment was to point this telebioscope at our own planet Earth. The data collected showed that the whole planet is not only alive, but that it possesses all the essential characteristics of a single living organism.

From these findings, one of the NASA scientists, James Lovelock, developed what he called the Gaia hypothesis, which proposes that our planet is a single living organism that maintains its own homeostasis. Lovelock noted that a slim margin of biophysical conditions on this planet allow life, as we know it, to exist. These biophysical conditions include a delicate stabilization of the chemical composition of the atmosphere, a ratio of mixtures of barometric pressures, heat from the sun, the axis spin rate, and the mineral composition of the ocean. If these, or many other variables that maintain life on this planet, are shifted more than a slight amount, life on this planet, as we know it, would end. Lovelock determined that these conditions necessary to maintain life on the planet are not inherently stable and that under the normal laws of physics and chemistry these conditions should have only lasted a short time. Somehow, through God's grace, something on this planet has been self-regulating and maintaining the equilibrium of these life-giving conditions for the last four billion years. We see this similar sort of homeostatic equilibrium in the human body. Perhaps the earth is alive! Perhaps we are each equivalent to one cell in this living organism!

The Gaia hypothesis—that planet Earth is a single living organism with intelligence and purpose—is both new and quite old. Ancient cultures often regarded the energies of the earth—all life, all minds, and the cosmos—as one, and yet, at the same time multiple manifestations of universal energy. This "new discovery" of the Gaia hypothesis supports our small but growing rediscovery of the unity of humanity and nature. One of the most exciting movements today is the tremendous groundswell of interest in national and international ecological concerns. In the last few years, so many ecologically oriented organizations and worldwide television programs have emerged that it is difficult to list them all, but many are included in the resources list in this book. The more we get in touch with the law of unity, the more we will be able to realize that the basic foundation for a healthy humanity is peace with nature.

To preserve the planet is to affirm our own divine spirit. It is the

affirmation of life—our very own life and meaning. A possible first step in moving back into alignment with our oneness with the living planet is to spend some quiet time in nature to feel our connection and then make the commitment, not just to be a steward of the living planet but to make a covenant to see oneself as part of the living planet as an expression of the Divine. And then let this new consciousness gently guide your actions and way of life to best honor this covenant.

CHAPTER 8

PEACE WITH THE RADIANT ONE

If we say the Heavenly Father
Dwelleth within us,
Then are the heavens ashamed;
If we say he dwelleth without us,
It is a falsehood.
The eye which scanneth the far horizon
And the eye which seeth the hearts of men,
He maketh as one eye.
He is not manifest,
He is not hidden.
He is not revealed,
Nor is he unrevealed.
My children, there are no words
To tell that which he is. ...
He who hath found peace
With his Heavenly Father
Hath entered the Sanctuary
Of the Holy Law. ...
For in the beginning was the Law,
And the Law was with God,
And the Law was God.
May the Sevenfold Path of Peace
Of the Heavenly Father
Be with thee always.

Essene Gospel of Peace, Book 2

PEACE WITH GOD IS TOTAL PEACE. It is the totality of the six aspects of peace combined with the transcendental awareness of the One. Peace with God is the indescribable caress of the Divine that we experience in the depth of our soul. It comes from a deep love communion with God. In divine communion, we become aligned with cosmic consciousness unfolding on this planet. This awareness manifests as harmony and love on every level of one's life. This state of awareness adds great depth and quality to any world service that we embrace. It enhances our ability to see God in every situation.

The fruition of the other levels of peace are both the cause and effect of this seventh, all-encompassing level of peace. Moving toward this profound level of peace is enhanced by an integration of efforts, such as eating an appropriate diet for a spiritual life, meditation, exercising, associating with people who are actively developing their spiritual awareness, starting all our thoughts with love, actively serving the cause of peace, experiencing the great works of culture, and communing with the forces of nature.

These efforts to develop ourselves gradually bring peace with the body and mind. From the base of a peaceful body and mind, and by keeping our hearts open to the vulnerability of intimacy, we develop peace with the family. Peace with humanity naturally develops when there is peace with the body, mind, and family. As our communion with the Divine develops, grace begins to make our efforts flow more easily and bear more fruit. **Peace with God gives meaning to the equation of our lives. It is the one in front of the zeroes that gives them value.**

CHAPTER 9

May Peace Prevail On Earth

INTEGRATING PEACE
ON EVERY LEVEL

Bring unto thy earth the reign of Peace!
Then shall we remember the words
Of him who taught of old the Children of Light:
I give the peace of the Earthly Mother to thy body,
And the peace of the Heavenly Father to thy spirit.
And let the peace of both reign among the sons of men. . . .
For happy are they that strive for peace,
For they will find the peace of the Heavenly Father,
And give to everyone thy peace,
Even as I have given my peace unto thee.
For my peace is of God.
Peace be with thee!

Essene Gospel of Peace, Book 3

THE SEVENFOLD PATH OF PEACE IS A PRACTICAL APPROACH
TO TOTAL PEACE. It is an active peace that we express on every level
to enhance the peace in our world and in ourselves. It entails living a
spiritual, yet practical, life in the world—not a passive, doormat, not-
rocking-the-boat, pseudo-peaceful life, but a life in which every action
is filled with integrity, love, compassion, and peace regardless of the
potential for rejection. The peaceful life is not necessarily easy at this
time in history. Mahatma Gandhi felt a life of nonviolent peacefulness
required more courage than any other. A peacemaker turns every moment
into an experience of harmony and peace. When we are serving peace,

we actively create peace with ourselves, with the family, with humanity, and with the total planetary organism. Serving peace means we feel complete union with all that is.

Even if we are graced with only a few minutes each day of this synergistic peace experience, it is more than enough. A high-level peace exists when there is a balance between the nondual merging in the Divine Communion in which we lose our Self and let go of body-consciousness, and the practical self-consciousness and body-consciousness that we need in order to operate physically in the world. In our lives today, most of us have become self-centered and separate beyond the safety point necessary to preserve the life of our physical instrument. This unnecessary separation from God within ourselves and others creates a feeling of lack because we do not experience the noncausal joy of Divine Communion. This limited reality of separation and duality consciousness deprives us from experiencing the abundance of the universe, the source of all material and spiritual resources, and love itself. This "I" and "thine" approach creates a fundamental disharmony in our relationship to every aspect of life on this planet and in this universe. In this state of disharmony, we mistakenly think we need to conquer and dominate to survive, rather than live by the abundance created from love. **The unity awareness of the Sevenfold Path of Peace helps us to shift away from this excessive self-centeredness to the peaceful dance of love with all of creation. In this state, there is no lack; there is only abundance for all of the earth and its creatures. The Essenes, who lived this way as a culture, always experienced abundance.**

The Sevenfold Path of Peace is not simply an intellectual construct. It is an active, daily practice of contemplation and action. It is an active effort to apply the wisdom of the mind and love of the heart to our social, cultural, earthly, and cosmic world. To the Essenes, harmony meant peace. The goal of the Sevenfold Path of Peace is to create harmony in all seven potential levels of peace in our lives. World peace will come faster if the Sevenfold Path of Peace is directly lived in our own immediate hearts, lives, and environment. There is no contradiction between manifesting the Sevenfold Path of Peace in our personal lives and working to bring the world into harmony by specific political efforts to improve the world through social action on behalf of the ecology, human rights, and anti-nuclear movements if our actions are guided by the feeling-prayer of noncausal peace, noncausal joy, and noncausal love. The important point, however, is that for peace to be lasting we must go beyond simply working against something done by the "bad guys." The integrated awareness of the Sevenfold Path of Peace supports us in not becoming caught in this dualistic trap. Working on these different levels of peace goes on simultaneously as we evolve. It is not like constructing a building, where one has to build each floor completely before going on to the next. Gently, and with time, our own contradictions and lack of harmony will be examined and brought into harmony as we move into walking between the nothing and something, and thus holding the nondual or Tree of Life consciousness as the inner guide to living in the dual, Tree-of-Good-and-Evil consciousness of the material world. To live in the synchronistically nondual/dual consciousness reflects a high level of God-awareness. In this way we become the expression of the Divine in the world. Although integrating the Sevenfold Path of Peace on every level does feel good, the human species still seems to have a resistance to peace.

Resistance to Peace

When physicist J. Robert Oppenheimer was asked by a congressional committee what we had to do to avoid a nuclear war, he answered clearly, "Make peace." Why do we still ponder the obvious? Why does creating peace on the planet and in our personal lives seem so complicated? Why, in 1988, was the peace effort in the United States considered one of the ten most underreported stories by the San Francisco-based Media Alliance? Why did people use the fear of a communist conspiracy in the fifties and sixties and terrorism in the current era, since 1990, to justify acting directly or indirectly against peace? And how is a generalized fear amplified by a fear of terrorism to undermine the vibration of peace? Why do some even invoke the name of God in their resistance to the worldwide peace movement? Why is peace not attractive? Novelist and Holocaust survivor Elie Wiesel, who won the Nobel Peace Prize in 1986, has at least part of the answer to these questions:

> Like the patient who dreads leaving his hospital bed, like the prisoner afraid of being taken from his familiar cell, we hesitate, waver: What is at risk is too important. We are afraid to let ourselves go, to allow ourselves to be carried away by wishful thinking.

Lasting peace, to some, seems unreal, a mere flowery concept to which we have aspired for centuries. Even some of us who talk about peace believe on a subtle level that it is *not* possible. The Institute for Noetic Sciences has pointed out that collectively held unconscious beliefs shape the world's institutions. A collective belief in the possibility of achieving harmonious global peace in our generation contributes to reaching this goal, just as our present collective disbelief thwarts it. **It is important that we create the belief in the possibility of peace within ourselves if we are to communicate it to others.**

A fundamental cause for the resistance to peace is an inability to see and experience the light of God in others because we either have forgotten the experience, or have not yet experienced that light in ourselves. If we do not know the love of the God Communion within ourselves, how can we love our neighbors as ourselves? Instead, we tend to mistreat our neighbors as we mistreat ourselves.

Another major underlying cause for war is our unconscious search to become whole through the transitory process of subjugating others, rather than through experiencing God Communion. This is the ego-based approach of the Culture of Death—"the more I have (material or power), the more I am." We often try to dominate others because we cannot risk seeing others as complete or fully human because then we might see ourselves as less than human. Dominating often comes from the a place of low self-esteem.

War allows us to create the illusion of personal wholeness by dehumanizing or subjugating others. As pointed out in a new and respected classic of social history, *The Chalice and the Blade* by Riane Eisler, war arises either from the need to subjugate others or the need to avoid subjugation. We do not seem to understand our real options for overcoming our sense of incompleteness. The idea of surviving or trying to feel better about ourselves at the expense of others results from this warlike way of thinking.

The work by René Girard, on violence and the sacred, adds to this understanding. Due to a "mimetic" or imitative desire, human beings, Girard argues, become addicted to competing with each other to fulfill artificially instilled desires. The drive to fulfill these desires is another form of trying to feel whole by conquest in the outer world. In this process of competition for our desires, we lose the sense of our oneness. From the consciousness of the Culture of Life and Liberation, this sense of separation and competition is classic thinking of the Culture of Death. As subsocieties, whole societies, or even nations, we regard each other as obstacles to the gratification of our desires. A meltdown of the social order begins when law and custom cannot contain the hostility. Historically, the way groups or nations have handled this is by the mechanism of scapegoating. The scapegoat can be an individual person—for example, the "identified patient" we may sometimes see in family dynamics—the one the family identifies as the "sick" one, and who is the cause of problems and pain in a family, rather than the one who is expressing the pain of the family. The scapegoat can include a whole culture, as was the case of the Jews in Germany, or the anti-Semitism and racism that arise in times of economic stress. Scapegoating may result in legitimized and actual human sacrifice. Although explicit human sacrifice is taboo, through the process of moral justification, it creeps back into our daily history. The Islamic terrorists, with their televised beheadings, have reintroduced the primitive practice of human sacrifice, as an active and socially accepted expression of the Culture of Death. Two major forms of the human sacrificial cult that are not recognized as such are war and the execution of criminals. These forms allow social anonymity in the participation in actual human sacrifice and usually serve to bring society back into "unity." By proclaiming their moral guilt, as is easy to do with criminals, or the fabricated moral culpability of the "communists" of the Cold War, or of anyone who stands in the way of what we want—for example, the possible Viet Cong among the villagers of the infamous My Lai massacre, or suicide bombing in Iraq and around the world, to justify the mass human sacrifice that occurred in these places, or the drug-dealing evil of a Noriega, or the genocidal evil of Saddam Hussein, or our historical witch hunts resulting in the Salem witch burnings, along with crusades, racist hangings, or pogroms, we become morally anesthetized to our actual practice of human sacrifice. This only works, however, when people accept the legitimacy of the cult of human sacrifice as the way to solve the problem of desire, rivalry, and internal social disunity. When we understand that the path to wholeness of the individual or the a nation is not through the temporary mechanism of scapegoating of an individual, a culture, or nation, then this cultic pseudo-solution will no longer work. When human sacrifice is no longer allowed to be "prime time," it will be a sign that our society is no longer willing to become anesthetized by the surface scapegoat thinking that the media subjects us to, such as the idea that to move toward peace we must "kill to stop the killing," or the fabricated or real moralistic impugning of a targeted scapegoat to "justify" the human sacrifice, as with the invasion of Iraq. **The task of the peacemaker is to live in a way that undermines the legitimacy of sacrificial cults and their mob psychology. As peacemakers, we must also live in a personal way that demonstrates that the long-term path to wholeness does not consist of subjugating or sacrificing our neighbors.**

Fortunately, we are beginning to recognize that the pattern of unconsciously searching for wholeness through dominating others is dysfunctional on a personal, national, and global level. We are becoming less willing to participate in actions that do not promote real wholeness and well-being. **Our paradigm of the Culture of Life and Liberation is shifting toward establishing real paths to wholeness and well-being that do not depend on the illusory and short-lived means of subjugating others. For this reason, we will all eventually become the Sevenfold Path of Peace.**

Just as overt legalized discrimination and slavery became obsolete because these practices no longer promoted the feeling of well-being for the majority, so a paradigm shift is emerging toward democracy and civil rights as a basic fundamental human right. In 2007 stands for peace by secular and monastic Burmese were seen around the world with more support than ever before; the paradigm of repression was seen to shift toward human rights. In 1989 the world was outraged at the Chinese leadership for slaughtering thousands of students in Tiananmen Square who were advocating for civil rights and democracy. This is in contrast to a much slower and quieter world reaction to the Chinese Cultural Revolution in the 1960s, in which millions were killed or imprisoned. Eastern Europe's sunburst of light toward establishing independent national democracies is an example of this thought-form change. Although these events do not guarantee the establishment of peace, because they primarily represent a political and economic shift toward civil rights rather than a sevenfold shift, they do represent a big step.

It is not so easy to feel whole, to open to the experience of God Communion, to keep our hearts open to love unconditionally, and to operate in the consciousness of the Sevenfold Path of Peace in our daily lives. For some, it may seem easier to avoid trying to achieve this feeling of wholeness rather than risk failure. Fortunately, in our personal and international relationships, we are beginning to recognize that it is dysfunctional to keep pursuing the illusion of wholeness through subjugating or overpowering others. At this point in history, our challenge is to become true wholeness. Some, however, are afraid of the experience of the light of the Divine within. For some of us, just the experience of being quiet may be threatening, because in those quiet moments we often fear we will get in touch with some parts of ourselves we do not want to experience. Others of us fear the inner world because it is uncharted and undefined. Still others are afraid of the immensity and expansive universal feeling of wholeness. Because we have never known this primary nurturing experience of the Divine, there are some of us who do not believe it is possible.

Many others have lost touch with the mystical experience of oneness and wholeness. When faced with the possibility of inner silence, it seems easier to start a "holy" crusade than to face the fear of the inner experience. It is as if a conditioned fear reflex gets activated that covers up our essential experience of wholeness with God. The author sees this all the time in participants at the Tree of Life. These programs are designed to stimulate the awakening to Divine Communion and the Sevenfold Path of Peace. One can often feel the resistance in people; sometimes it's an absolute terror of letting go, although often it is just hesitation about surrendering to a greater awareness than our limiting ego. In the author's own preliminary awakening in 1972, there was an agonizing hour filled with fear of the mystical unknown. This experience has made it easier for the author to recognize it in others. Once this fear of the silence and the unknown within it is acknowledged, it is amazing how easily and quickly most people, with just a little support, pass through it in a few minutes or hours. If we do not acknowledge the fear and directly face it, it sometimes takes a longer time to break through—or it may not happen at all.

One of the most basic resistances to peace is human inertia. Many people do not value peace enough to want to make the effort necessary to bring about inner changes. Who likes to give up their comforts? It is, indeed, uncomfortable in some ways to change one's lifestyle. This is especially true when we do not feel any direct pain from it, such as a cigarette smoker or coffee drinker often does not immediately have this direct pain in the moment. Peace is not perceived as a dramatic or urgent issue, like a famine in Africa, or a tsunami hitting Indonesia. It is easy not to make it an active priority in our lives. The inertia manifests even with something relatively "painless," like adopting the peaceful practice of a vegetarian diet, which directly helps to save the rainforests and preserve the ecology, or living in other ways that will support planetary survival.

Creating peace requires an effort by all of us to overcome our inertia, even on what seems the smallest level. In southern California, people complained when the anti-pollution program went beyond stricter control of industries and auto pollution into their own backyards. They did not like it when their polluting gasoline-powered lawn mowers and barbecues were included. In the San Francisco Bay Area, the *San Francisco Chronicle* reported that it took a U.S. District Judge to order a crackdown on pollution caused by household products such as cleaners, aerosols, deodorants, insect sprays, furniture polishes, and air fresheners. Because the reductions in the use of household pollutants in the San Francisco Bay Area were to be made by 1985, the judge castigated state officials for their "appalling failure" to act sooner and gave them until 1993 to reduce consumer polluting solvents by four tons a day. Honestly acknowledging our resistance to the changes needed for a more peaceful lifestyle allows us to boldly face our inertia and inspire ourselves to overcome it.

Developing the heartfelt willingness to share the resources of the world in some more equal way between the haves and have-nots is even more threatening. Our greedy, automaton desires to hang onto our addictions and to the familiar ways that bring direct and indirect violence to ourselves and the rest of the planet create a tremendous resistance to peace. **Living peacefully on every level is not necessarily easy, but it is profoundly worth it. There are great subtle rewards when we change our lifestyle habits away from those that directly or indirectly support a warlike attitude or actions of the Culture of Death toward humanity and the planet. There is an opening up and a freeing of energy; a joy emerges that makes us come alive and makes our lives intensely meaningful when we begin to live fully in love and peace in the Culture of Life and Liberation.**

WAYS TO OVERCOME INERTIA AND MAKE PEACE

Institutions alone cannot save the earth from the cumulative results of our everyday, seemingly unimportant inner thoughts and lifestyle actions or lack of actions. Sometimes we feel helpless in the face of the apparent power of governments or large corporations. But remember, governments and corporations are made up of people, and they depend on people for their power. We are those people. Our seemingly unimportant thoughts and actions *do* make a difference. Our collective daily choices about how we live on this planet in a continual feeling prayer of peace, love, and compassion have a profound impact. Someday, if we all participate in changing our own lives, we will make a significant difference, and peace will prevail on earth.

Peace with the Body

Choose to take responsibility for your own personal health and improve the ecology of your personal body just as you would care for the planet. (a) Exercise aerobically at least three times per week for one-half hour. (b) Since 90 percent of our energy comes from oxygen, practice deep breathing at least once a day with ten cycles of a seven-count in and seven-count out deep breath. (c) Get sufficient sleep and relaxation. (d) Drink sufficient pure water.

Peace with the planetary body: (a) If you are not a vegetarian already, read *Diet for a New America* by John Robbins and *Conscious Eating* by the author, and consider the ramifications of eating flesh food on the planetary ecology and peace in general. The flesh-food industry accounts for more than 50 percent of our water usage, 85 percent of soil loss, and approximately sixteen times more land usage than that required for a vegan diet. (b) At your own rate, add vegetarian food and progressively cut red meat, poultry, and fish from your diet. (c) Support local farmers' markets; their produce usually has less pesticide residue and is fresher.

(d) Buy certified organically grown produce on a regular basis. All of this preserves bodily health, soil fertility, and wildlife, and minimizes soil loss and water pollution. By choosing to eat a plant-source-only cuisine, not only do we create peace with the body, but create peace with the mind, family, humanity, and all cultures including the Animal Kingdom, the ecology, and ultimately peace with the Radiant One.

Peace with the cosmic body: Think of yourself as one cell in the cosmic body. **Instead of thinking about humanity as the web of life, begin to understand humanity as one strand in the *cosmic* web of life.**

Peace with the Mind

Enhance your own inner peace by learning to meditate or pray, and do it on a daily basis. Keep asking, do I "barter that which is eternal for that which dieth in an hour?"

Enhance peace with the planetary mind by thinking positive thoughts and participating in some peace group thought-form activity such as World Healing Hour on December 31st, Peace the 21st on each equinox or solstice, or on the last day of the month. Or become a daily participant in the Peace Every Day Initiative by becoming a living-feeling prayer of peace, love, and compassion at sunrise and sunset, and eventually all the time.

Enhance peace with the cosmic mind by trying to begin each thought, word, and action with love, compassion, and peace.

Peace with the Family

Forgive everybody. Forgiveness ends the negative memory and dispels the energy of conflict. **Forgiveness is the blessing of living peace.**

Love your neighbor as your divine self. If you are not sure whether you or your neighbor have a divine self, pretend that both of you do and try relating from that understanding.

The power of becoming a feeling prayer of peace is that it allows us to activate the hologram of peace that exists somewhere in every person and in every family, tribe, and culture.

Peace with Humanity

Make a point to volunteer or contribute to humanitarian causes and organizations. Check with any local peace center for a list of causes and ways to contribute. Volunteers are much appreciated by almost all of these groups. See the resources list in this book for ideas.

Develop your livelihood so that it supports or expresses your personal and planetary peace values. Start this one step at a time. It may take several years, so be patient and persistent.

Begin socially responsible investing (SRI)—investing in organizations with positive community and environmental policies. Get a credit card, mutual fund, and/or a checking account with an SRI policy. For information on SRI companies, ask your investment counselor, bank, or credit union.

Become a peacemaker in all levels of your life and inspire others to do the same. Let your life be an example of living your ideals. The cumulative effect of inspiring your friends, and your friends inspiring a wider circle, will transform our social, economic, governmental, and religious institutions and bring peace to the world.

Peace with Culture

Participate in art, music, drama, or other cultural events that inspire and connect you with the eternal values of love, peace, beauty, truth, and the Divine in all.

Make peace with your own cultural roots. Ask your parents or grandparents for stories about your cultural origins. Read a book about them or take a class on your culture of origin.

Try to find and appreciate the flourishing of peace and joy in all cultures.

Explore activities that bring you into harmony with the culture of nature's rhythms. It is not surprising that most cultures have such rituals.

Use knowledge about the Culture of Death to inspire yourself to

reach new understanding and expression of the Culture of Life and Liberation.

Peace with Nature, or the Living Ecology

Commit yourself to planting one or more trees this year. According to *50 Simple Things You Can Do to Save the Earth,* the average American consumes the equivalent of seven trees per year. It also points out that if every American family planted one tree per year, more than a billion pounds of "greenhouse gases" would be removed from the air per year. Planting seven trees each year would keep us ecologically even. Because trees absorb large quantities of carbon dioxide, they help to prevent the greenhouse effect, provide oxygen, help to preserve the soil, and are uplifting to the spirit. The practices of planting trees, cover crops, and grasses, composting, or organic farming to make up for our modern lifestyle, which creates global warming emissions, together are called carbon sequestering. The more plants one puts in the ground, the more healthy the soil one creates, and the more carbon preservation. By creating businesses that promote carbon sequestering, we protect the planet from degrading and global warming.

Recycle all newspapers, glass, aluminum, tin, organic refuse, and anything else you are able to recycle creatively. Recycling has a powerful conservation effect on our environment. If everyone in the United States recycled even one-tenth of their newspapers, we would save about 25 million trees per year. **Small individual steps multiplied by millions do make a difference.**

Support environmental groups by volunteering or with donations.

Participate in the "campaign for the earth," which is a unifying symbolic idea, not an organization, for individuals and groups around the world committed to working to heal the planet and ourselves as part of that process. The campaign involves acting as part of the vision of healing the earth. Identify with the vision through your own unique action and thoughts. Share the vision with others. Acknowledge yourself as a citizen of the earth and one with the living planet as an expression of the Divine.

Read and act on *50 Simple Things You Can Do to Save the Earth* or similar sources of ideas.

Peace with God

Find your own personal way to connect with the Divine every day.

Allow yourself to express in the world as the living will and flow of the Divine.

THE FULL PEACE OF WHOLENESS

Although the essence of most spiritual teachings gives a message of the importance of turning within, most people have been programmed to believe that the way to attain happiness, and therefore peace, is through some sort of external achievement. Some form of domination is involved in striving for success, whether it's by accumulating lots of money and external trophies of material achievement, winning in athletic competition, rising to the top of the corporation or union, winning political elections, winning a war, subduing the environment, shopping, or controlling other people in relationships or through organizational structures. These approaches may work for a little while. As a former captain of an undefeated college football team, the author remembers how good it felt to dominate another team. The author recalls how hard he would work to win again the next week so he could again feel good, or at least not feel bad. Spectators are one step removed from the same process of trying to feel whole through the victories of their team. Sometimes, for example, in the Superbowl or hometown college football games, the spectators get as "high" about the game as the players. One day the author simply woke up and saw this endless conscious-unconscious search for an external event to make himself feel whole for the illusion that it was, and he stopped. This does not mean that the author melted forever into an inactive, blissful lump on the floor. He continues to be as active as before, but now is primarily guided by the unfolding of the divine will on the planet expressing through his physical, emotional, mental, and spiritual form.

Many experts now call us a nation of addicts. Our affluent culture has found many external ways to, at least temporarily, relieve the feeling of discontent and lack of wholeness. Overeating and drugs are just two of the more predominant ways. But it is not just drugs, food, relationships, or other forms of anesthetizing ourselves in our comfort zone to which we are addicted; at its source we are addicted to the search for the experience of peace and wholeness. Our addictions arise because we are involved in an endless repetitious array of external activities in an effort to attain a permanent experience of peace and happiness. The problem is that peace, happiness, and wholeness cannot be found on a permanent basis through external activities. For example, one cannot eat one's way to God. **There is never enough food to feed a hungry soul, so no matter how much one eats or how overweight one becomes, the soul that feels empty remains empty. The real nourishment of the soul comes from opening one's soul to the light of the Radiant One.**

Peace, happiness, and wholeness require a shift from external manipulation to the internal quest. A true story was shared with the author by someone who realized this point through a series of experiences. After he finished the excitement of athletics in college, he began to feel empty and bored. To alleviate this, he took up motorcycle riding, which gave him some temporary happiness. When that didn't work anymore, he took up downhill skiing, which made him feel okay for a few years. When skiing stopped working for him, he went in for skydiving. This worked for a while until he broke both legs in a poor landing. At this point, he decided there must be a more direct way to feel happy and whole. His search led him to experience the Divine in meditation. Saint Augustine, in his autobiography *The Confessions,* describes this moment of change: "Thou hast made us for thyself, O Lord, and our hearts are restless until they rest in thee."

The source from which all peace grows is our experience of the Divine in our lives. Many people first experience the Divine within; then, as a seed grows, it permeates our outer experience. Others first begin to develop a process of sacramental awareness (sense of the holy) in which the boundary between outer and inner lessens through meditation on scriptures, nature, persons, or events. This experience of wholeness brings a spontaneously arising contentment, inner calm, tranquility, and harmony with, and as, the One. This awareness cannot be fully communicated. Each person experiences it in his or her own way and language.

The experience of Divine Communion entails a feeling of total, abundant fullness with the Divine. A person with such an awareness lives a life that is full of the sweet presence of the Divine with every breath. He or she is made sublimely content with the daily kiss of all the angels of the earth and heavens. Love pulses in every bodily cell, nurtured by the essential peace of all creation. The energies of all the forces of life tingle through the body with a quiet excitement; they flow through the body in the exquisite harmony of the One as we live our daily lives. A joy bubbles from the heart. **With every breath, with every sound, with every moment, the one at peace is bathed in the inner nectar of love. A life of peace is fun.**

As the great Sufi poet Rumi put it:

> The man of God is drunken [God-intoxicated] while sober. The man of God is full without meat [food].

The more we experience this subtle "intoxication," the more it becomes a sustained awareness in us. We meditate to reclaim the primary awareness that we are love, compassion, peace, and wholeness, and from this the rest of the peace work will follow naturally.

Isaiah 30:15 states, "In sitting still and rest shall you be saved, in quietness and confidence will be your strength." Prayer, good fellowship, and service with the awareness of the Divine in our brothers and sisters are also powerful ways to reclaim the primary experience of the One. The full practice of the consciousness of the Sevenfold Path of Peace is an important aid to this sustained experience of wholeness, because it was developed for bringing us into harmony. It is probably why the Essenes were able to sustain their communities in such profound peace for so many hundreds of years.

Practicing the Sevenfold Path of Peace

The Essenes contemplated one of the principles of the Sevenfold Path of Peace at noontime each day. On Saturday, they focused on transcendental awareness; on Sunday, peace with the kingdom of nature; on Monday, peace with culture; on Tuesday, peace with humanity, or social peace; on Wednesday, peace with the family; on Thursday, peace with the mind; and on Friday, peace with the body. On Saturday, in addition to focusing on the Divine, one of the other six aspects is also contemplated all day long.

The Sevenfold Path of Peace awareness cycle takes seven weeks. This gentle practice helps us to maintain a conscious awareness of the living of peace in our lives. To create peace for ourselves and this world requires some effort. Yet, paradoxically, total peace is not an automatic result of circumstances or practices. Total peace happens beyond the bonds of linear, causal process, through the intangibility of grace.

Conclusion

It is estimated that within the next few decades the deterioration of the earth's life support systems will accelerate at such a rate that none of our present mild efforts at conservation will be able to save us. In 2008, the estimates are becoming progressively alarming; the situation has become radical. In this case, moderation kills, and a far more radically committed set of internal and external actions are needed. The tropical forests that are our earth's lungs are too rapidly being destroyed, and the oceans, rivers, and waterways that are our earth's circulation system are becoming so polluted that the earth as an organism is becoming toxic. The flesh of our earthly topsoil is being scraped so thin that it will no longer be able to support us. We are like a global alcoholic who is unable to stop drinking as his body and mind deteriorate from the toxicity of the alcohol.

Will the people on this planet choose to be so attached to their destructive habits and consumptive lifestyle that they would rather die than give them up? Or, in an act of sanity and spiritual awareness, will there be a mass human awakening to our condition and to the need for peace on every level? Will we choose to sober up? Will we choose to wake up and heal ourselves on a global level? Nothing less than the full Sevenfold Path of Peace as an expression of the Culture of Life and Liberation is worth living at this time, because nothing less will be strong enough medicine to heal this planet and ourselves. What is necessary is a commitment, or a covenant with the living planet as an expression of God and with ourselves to become a living-feeling prayer of peace on every level in every moment.

As it says in the Essene Gospel of Peace, Book 2, in The Essene Book of Revelations, probably the early edition of Revelation to John, the apostle John is deeply saddened by the vision of the future he is shown. John seeks hope and his vision shifts from planetary death, destruction, and chaos to a different outcome.

> But I saw not what befell them, my vision changed, and I saw a new heaven and a new earth: for the first heaven and the earth were passed away … and I heard a great voice … saying, "There shall be no more death, … neither shall there be more pain."

The angel further says, "Nation shall not lift up sword against nation, neither shall they learn war anymore, for the former themes are passed away." The point to hold close to your heart is that by living life as a prayer of peace, we can change the outcome to one of joyous love and God Communion. It is up to us to affect the outcome. **If enough of us commit to be the new vision, we can do this also. And peace, love, and compassion will guide life on earth, so that heaven will reign on earth. In** prophecy, there are multiple outcomes in each time-space continuum; we can choose the most peaceful outcome, but only if we choose to *be* it.

The way of peace is to make peace the feeling prayer in every cell of our body and on all seven levels of our lives. At the same time, it requires us to commit to one genuine step at a time, to commit to actions we feel in our hearts that we can honestly make and sustain. To set goals for changes in ourselves that are beyond our capacity can lead to confusion and discouragement for ourselves and for those to whom we have made the commitments. For us to become peacemakers, we need the holy intention and self-will to overcome our own inertia, fear, and apathy toward creating peace. Our job, then, becomes to inspire people out of their apathy toward peace, to dispel ignorance, to overcome our subtle disbelief and fear of the experience of peace, to start every thought and action with love, compassion, and peace, and to bring this love and peace to every situation the best we can. To create peace in our own lives, our beliefs and the way we live must come into alignment. In this way we create peace by being peace.

Collectively we can and will, with God's grace, heal ourselves and the soul of this planet.

And all shall work together
In the garden of the Brotherhood
Yet each shall follow his own path
And each shall commune with his own heart.
Though the brothers be of different complexion
Yet do they all toil
In the vineyard of the Earthly Mother
And they all do lift their voice together
In praise of the Heavenly Father
There shall be no peace among peoples
Till there be one garden of the brotherhood
Over the earth.

Essene Gospel of Peace, Book 2

THE PEACE EVERY DAY INITIATIVE: MEDITATING DAILY TO CREATE PEACE BY BEING PEACE

WORLD PEACE—THE HEALING OF THE WORLD—IS ACHIEVED
THROUGH A VERY SIMPLE PRINCIPLE: WE CREATE PEACE BY
BEING PEACE. It is this universal truth that has inspired the Peace Every
Day Initiative, a global, collective, daily, meditation of peace. The purpose is to unite through conscious intention a minimum of 8,000 people,
while holding the vision of 144,000 or more people, to meditate-pray by
becoming a feeling-based prayer of peace for three minutes or more two
times each day, optimally at sunrise and sunset, but anytime is good. This
powerful thought form of peace is enough to begin to shift the global
consciousness so that we may fully celebrate peace on earth!

Launching the Initiative

Peace Every Day Initiative was launched on November 8, 2003 at sunset.
On this date was an astrological Harmonic Concordance, a lunar eclipse
and a six-planet configuration in the shape of the Star of David. The concordance is said to accelerate the healing of karma, heal the waters of the
planet, heal the ecosystem, elevate consciousness, and harmonize male
and female into sacred relationship, a subtle relationship that supports
people living in the Divine Presence. It was an accelerated opportunity
for humans to work collectively to enhance the transformation of the
planet.

It began by simply actualizing the practice of being peace by
meditating-praying at the time of sunrise and sunset and continuing
daily with the commitment. All are invited to make a commitment to

this matrix of peace at any time—so that the Peace Every Day Initiative may gain momentum.

Making the Commitment of Peace

In order that we may usher in the reign of peace, the Peace Every Day Initiative asks that each person who feels deeply connected to peace on earth make a commitment for a minimum of four years to be peace by meditating or praying for three minutes or more each day, five to seven days per week. Before the prayer, it is best to meditate to quieten the mind in order to become and sustain the vibration of peace. Whether meditating individually or praying in a group, we link worldwide to create an amplified force field of peace, love, and compassion. Although it may be true that sunrise or sunset, the two nodal times of the day, are the most effective times for the vibration of peace to be transmitted into the global mind, it is more important that in our daily gatherings, as peaceable beings, we practice the initiative no matter what the time is. Even for those who already have a daily meditation-prayer practice, your participation in the Peace Every Day Initiative without changing your existing practice, except to add three minutes of feeling-based prayer two times a day, is an act of making a conscious global action for creating peace.

Transforming Gatherings into Being Peace

Whether you gather for an instructional class on any topic, an organizational meeting, time in nature, support groups, afternoon social tea, or whatever—please choose to share the Peace Every Day Initiative as part of your getting together.

Honoring All Spiritual Paths

The Peace Every Day Initiative acknowledges the many people around the world that have a committed, daily meditation practice and honors all forms of meditation-prayer. The purpose of the Peace Every Day

Initiative is to create a global link in intention and consciousness so that each of our unique spiritual expressions can become strong threads woven together in the tapestry of peace. It is an opportunity to celebrate the spiritual unity of all peoples beyond the paradigms of culture, traditions, and spiritual paths while fully honoring their roots in our own lives. The Peace Every Day Initiative practice of creating peace by being peace is whatever form of meditation or prayer that is meaningful to you, whether it is Jewish, kabbalistic, Essene, Yogic, Christian, Islamic, Sikh, Buddhist, Native American, or any other spiritual path.

The Practice

The practice is to simply quieten the mind, and create a feeling-experience of peace. Meditation is a very common way of doing this that is harmonious with all spiritual paths. But for those who don't meditate-pray, you may simply visualize and experience yourself in the beauty of nature, with the sound of a bubbling stream, or birds chirping, or the silence of a tree. Any activity in which you are being peace for three minutes such as chanting, dancing, or sitting quietly is appropriate and appreciated. For those who have an established practice of meditation or prayer, the Peace Every Day Initiative fully honors that practice and does not ask that you alter your practice in order to participate in the initiative. Participation in the Peace Every Day Initiative is marked by linking together in one global consciousness through intention to create peace for three minutes two times each day.

During your peace practice, move into silence, and from that silence, be the thought, emotion, and feeling of complete peace in every cell in the body and every aspect of your being. Allow yourself to be the feeling-based experience of peace. Meditation itself, which is the effortless dissolving into the One is the fullest manifestation of this vibration of peace. Near the end of your meditation or peace practice, allow your consciousness to connect with the thousands of other souls on the planet who are being peace to form a vibrational grid of peace around the globe. Move into the awareness that the peace you are being has already happened globally, as if the world is already in the Thousand Years of Peace. Peace is now! Experience gratefulness, appreciation, and thankfulness to the Divine for this Thousand Years of Peace now happening.

Being Our Peace Prayer-Meditation

All forms of prayer-meditation with a sincere heart create a vibration of peace. Powerful, ancient teachings also support the understanding that in order to effectively usher in the new paradigm of peace through a group collective effort of prayer-meditation, it is important that we create a feeling-based prayer in which we are being our prayer. The ancient Essene-kabbalistic teaching has a specific word for this technology of prayer—*l'hitpallel*. It is a unique expression, profoundly different than the contemporary meaning of prayer that often infers praying to God or begging God to change God's mind (as if God is outside of us). L'hitpallel is a verb. It means to do something to change oneself to be the prayer. This way of being in prayer is also embodied in the Native American way as well as the Tibetan Buddhist and other traditions as well.

L'hitpallel is not simply about an external God hearing prayers; it is about us being our prayers, in other words, to hear our own prayers by being them. This is the key technology. We create a feeling of peace, rather than a prayer asking for peace. The prayer is powered by our intention. Prayers without heartfelt intention are like birds with broken wings; they do not fly anywhere. In l'hitpallel, we are actively and intentionally filling our hearts and having a feeling-based experience of what it is that we are creating. At the end of the prayer, the power of the prayer is enhanced by feeling that what we are praying for has already happened, and for this we stay in a state of thankfulness. To create peace we must change ourselves—becoming what it is that we wish to see in ourselves and in the world. When we change ourselves, we change the world. Feeling-based prayer puts into place the vibratory possibilities of a particular outcome—in this case, world peace. In other words, we create a collective resonance that becomes a holographic emanation and expression of peace, love, and compassion.

Being the Sevenfold Path of Peace

The peace process does not begin with politicians, nationalism, or world economic policies. It depends on us, the people, taking responsibility to create such a strong thought form and feeling of peace that the global mind shifts away from that of war consciousness to a global village of peace consciousness, from that of economic greed, competition, and domination to one of synergy and cooperation, from separation from the Divine and need to conquer nature to one of harmony with nature and humanity, from the concept of the accumulation of wealth and material resources as the purpose of life to one of synergy and cooperation and of receiving in order to share so that the whole planet may evolve spiritually. From the Essene tradition, peace is not an external political protocol; it is an active sevenfold process of creating peace, harmony, and love with the One—peace with the body, the mind, the spirit, one's family, society, the ecology of the living planet, and the Divine Presence. In this process, we create peace by being peace. It is from this place of inner peace that we have more energy and vision to be outer peace, to create the vibration that will sustain an outer peace.

The Global Mind

The global mind, although there are occasional sparks of peace through the efforts of many peaceworkers, is still dominated by the consciousness of fear, global greed, global economism, and war. Given this, how will lasting peace be effected? Since some people are willing to put so much effort and sacrifice into creating a global vibration of war for self-gain and global domination, in order to shift the global mind there needs to be an equal, daily, sustained effort in creating a global resonance of peace.

This global resonance will manifest more quickly as people from diverse backgrounds and religious and spiritual traditions are willing to come together in cooperation and unity, acting with an attitude of tolerance and love. **We actually become a living experience of peace. In this way, we realize what the Prophet Zechariah taught, "Not by might, and not by power, but by spirit alone" will we all live in peace.**

A Global Collective Effort

History shows us that it takes more than a few peace celebrations to sustain peace on earth. This is the time to step up the effort of our intention and become a continuous, active, global vibration of peace. The act of meditating-praying together is a powerful way for each of us to be the peace process. This technology for true world peace transformation—the healing of the world—already exists. All that is needed is enough people to participate in awakening to and sustaining this truth. The transformation to peace consciousness accelerates when there is a critical mass of the population that join together from all different walks of life, ages, spiritual and religious traditions, to pray and meditate—creating peace by being peace.

It has been hypothesized that as little as the square root of 1 percent of the world population, which is approximately 8,000 people, is enough to begin to shift the global mind into one of world consciousness for peace. It is for this reason that the Peace Every Day Initiative is committed to inspire at least 8,000 people to collectively create a powerful thought form of peace, every day. Our vision is that the number of people meditating collectively through consciousness and intention will soon surpass 144,000, a sacred number for the healing of the world that will bring the Thousand Years of Peace. May the initiative spread to include millions of committed peaceworkers worldwide. The presence of every single person makes a difference. Leviticus 26:8 says, "A hundred of you shall chase away ten thousand." This ancient truth of the power of uniting in peace, which has been with us for more than 3,400 years, now has some illuminating contemporary, scientific support.

Scientific Support for Collective Meditation-Prayer

The Peace Every Day Initiative has been deeply inspired and validated by many scientific research projects that clearly demonstrate the power and effectiveness of group meditation-prayer for creating peace. The idea that a critical mass of meditators being peace in a specific population area can create positive social change has been supported by more than 300 studies. For example, in 1973, Dilbeck and Associates found in twenty-two similar cities, with populations of approximately 25,000, in half of those cities, where 1 percent of the population was practicing Transcendental Meditation™, there was an average of 16 percent less crime. In a similar study, 350 TM meditators were brought in for a period of three months in the state of Rhode Island. Researchers observed that there was a more than 43 percent drop in social disorder, including suicides, homicides, divorce, traffic fatalities, rapes, robbery, aggravated assaults, and larceny, and even a drop in beer and cigarette sales. After the meditators left, the statistics for social disorder went back to "normal." In order to prove that this drop of 43 percent was not a fluke, the TM meditators repeated the same experiment the next summer, and found a similar drop in the statistics of social disorder.

Group prayer and meditation not only affect the consciousness of people toward peace, but research by Dr. Buryl Payne, on the solar effects of the Peace the 21st world peace meditations each equinox and solstice, shows that we even affect the whole solar system. In studying sunspot activity around the time of the Peace the 21st meditations, he found an average of 36 percent decrease in sunspot activity for the following four days after each meditation. His previous statistical research points out that a decrease in sunspot activity is associated with more social harmony on earth.

Physicists have discovered, also, that the principle of critical mass is seen in nature. They have found that in the use of laser technology, when eight of sixty-four random photons become synchronized, the other fifty-six random photons spontaneously become synchronized in a laser form. Again we see support for the principle that when the square root is coherent it brings coherence to the larger whole.

Two sets of research done at the HeartMath Institute have further clarified the power of the feeling-based prayer. Their researchers found two sets of information: (1) When DNA is placed in a vacuum, it creates a subtle energy field template that organizes the photon patterns, and even when the DNA is taken away, the photon pattern remains. (2) Researchers found that our emotional state creates an electromagnetic field that extends at least fifty feet, affecting leaves, trees, and all of nature. This research clearly documents the relationship between feelings and the physical world. **In other words, human thought and emotion create a feeling that literally organizes the arrangement and frequency of our cellular DNA. Our DNA gives off a frequency that arranges and affects the molecular structures, both inside our body, creating health or illness, and outside our body.** Therefore, as we change our emotions and thoughts, we create a feeling that changes the DNA. This change in DNA changes the consciousness pattern outside of ourselves in all of nature, including us human beings and our consciousness, as we are a part of nature. By this state of our consciousness we have the opportunity to create a social matrix of peace that can heal the planet.

As pointed out by the Peace Every Day Initiative (PEDI) founder, Gabriel Cousens, MD, in his book *Spiritual Nutrition: Six Foundations for Spiritual Life and the Awakening of Kundalini,* we are living human crystals, and the heart and brain are huge liquid crystals that give off powerful electromagnetic fields. Researchers have since found that there is a five- to eight-foot electromagnetic field extending from the human body around the heart that they have measured. It may actually extend for miles. The heart gives off a field that regulates the brain, and the brain then sends the message to our DNA, which transmits to all of creation. As illustrated by Buryl Payne's research, this field goes beyond fifty feet to literally affect at least the solar system. It has long been known that electromagnetic fields in nature can affect barometric pressure, and that the electromagnetic fields of humans in group prayer can create rain or tornadoes. Once, with Swami Muktananda in South Fallsburg, New York, there was a concern about a drought in Texas. The group, including Gabriel, meditated for it to rain in Texas. Well, first it rained on us, which was not exactly what we expected, and then it rained the next day in Texas. We can create rain and we can create a reign of peace.

The "Silent Minute"

There are many testaments to the powerful effects of collective meditation-prayer. The "Silent Minute" is a historic example of the victory of this effort. The concept of the Silent Minute each day was developed in Britain during World War II. People were asked to devote one minute of prayer for peace at nine o'clock each evening. This dedicated minute received the support of King George, Sir Winston Churchill, and his Cabinet. It was also recognized by President Roosevelt and observed on land and sea, on battlefields, in air raid shelters, and in hospitals. With Churchill's support, the BBC, on Sunday, November 10, 1940, began to play the bells of Big Ben on the radio as a signal for the Silent Minute. This continued daily from 1942 to the end of the war, totaling millions of people.

An interesting anecdote emphasizes the profound power of the group meditation of the Silent Minute. In 1945, a British intelligence officer was interrogating a high Nazi official. He asked him why he thought Germany lost the war. His reply was, "During the war, you had a secret weapon for which we could find no countermeasure, which we did not understand, but it was very powerful. It was associated with the striking of the Big Ben each evening. I believe you called it the 'Silent Minute.'"

The Need for a Daily Commitment

The question one asks as a peaceworker is, "Why haven't our collective peace efforts created a lasting shift . . . yet?" Research on this question by the Transcendental Meditation organization was that the effect of group meditation begins to fade approximately three weeks after the critical mass is no longer actively meditating in an area. This is why it is necessary at this point to go beyond a single worldwide event, four big events a year, monthly events, and even weekly meditation groups, to bring the process of inner and outer peace to a daily experience of creating peace by being peace.

Registering Your Commitment

For those who are willing to make this profound commitment of meditating daily for peace, we would appreciate if you would register on the Peace Every Day website, www.peaceeveryday.org. (Your e-mail address will only be used to notify you of the progress of this project. It will not be available for any other purpose.) Our aim is to catalog that we have reached the vision of 8,000/144,000 or more people meditating collectively through the unity of consciousness each day. If you are the leader of a large group of people committed to a daily practice of prayer-meditation, you may register on behalf of your entire group by simply telling us the number of committed people in your group. (Thus they do not also register individually.)

We hope that those who already have a dedicated practice of prayer and meditation, as well as those who are new to this form of invoking peace, will register. An important part of the initiative is to learn how many people worldwide are meditating—thereby holding the vibration of peace. As the initiative grows, the website will allow you to discover how many people have committed to the Peace Every Day Initiative, the practice of daily meditation, to be a living, feeling-based prayer of peace, love, and compassion, and also support those who wish to connect with others in their local area to form Peace Every Day Initiative meditation groups.

Blessings

May you be blessed for your choice to consciously cooperate in the healing of yourself and the healing of the soul of the world.

Rebbe Gabriel Cousens, MD, MD(H), Diplomate of the American Board of Holistic Medicine, Diplomate in Ayurveda

www.peaceeveryday.org

The full expression of Gabriel's work can be explored through the Tree of Life website, www.treeoflife.nu, and www.gabrielcousens.com

Peace prevails on Earth!

Co-Sponsors of Peace Every Day Initiative

Many peace groups and spiritual leaders have committed to meditating daily as peace.

I honor the Peace Every Day Initiative.

His Holiness the Dalai Lama

I applaud the Peace Every Day Initiative with all my heart.

John Hagelin, Founder, Permanent Peace

To bring peace on Earth, let everyone meditate Peace Every Day.

Jose Arguelles-Valum Votan, President, Foundation for the Law of Time

Rev. Michael Beckwith, Agape Spiritual Center (agapelive.com) and Association for Global New Thought (agnt.org)

Ahmed Kostas, Director of Islamic Affairs, Kingdom of Morocco

Rabbi Michael Lerner, the Tikkun Community (www.tikkun.org) and the Network of Spiritual Progressives (www.spiritualprogressives.org)

Neale Donald Walsch, founder of Humanity's Team, www.humanitysteam.com

Jivamukti Yoga, co-founded by Sharon Gannon and David Life, www.jivamuktiyoga.com

Gregg Braden, author of *The Lost Mode of Prayer, The Divine Matrix,* and *The God Code,* www.greggbraden.com

Guardians of the Tradition of the Prophet Mohammed (ANSAR ASSUNA), Ghassan Manasra

Rabbi Zalman Schachter-Shalomi, www.yesodfoundation.org

Gurmukh Kaur Khalsa, Director of Golden Bridge Yoga, www.goldenbridgeyoga.com

Spirit Voyage, Snatam Kaur Celebrate Peace Tour, www.spiritvoyage.com

Dharma Singh Khalsa, MD, author of *Meditation as Medicine,* drdharma.com/prayer_community.htm

Wolfgang Bernard, Awakening from the Illusion of Identity, www.finaldialogue.com

Institute of Noetic Sciences, www.noetic.org

Amit Goswami, PhD, author of *The Quantum Book of Living and Dying* and *How Consciousness Creates the World*

Yogi Amrit Desai, www.amrityoga.org

Robert Muller, founder of World Core Curriculum, former. U.N. Assistant Secretary General, www.robertmuller.com

Sri Karunamayi, www.karunamayi.org

Creating Peace by Being Peace is exactly what the Gandhi Institute is working to achieve, with people supporting each other. . . . I gladly endorse the Peace Every Day Initiative.

Arun Gandhi, Gandhi Institute

Sant Mat, www.knowthyselfassoul.net and www.santmat.org

Richard Moss, MD, www.richardmoss.com

Foundation for Conscious Evolution, www.barbaramarxhubbard.org

Planet Coexist/C.A.R.E., www.planetcoexist.com

The New Century Foundation, www.NCFinternational.org

Tantra Yoga International, www.tantrayogainternational.org

Michael Ratner, Peace Conference and Friendship Fellowship, www.PeaceConference.org

Go Gratitude Experiment, www.gogratitude.com

Steven Sadleir, www.selfawareness.com

Dancing Freedom, Dharma Dancing, Archana Samantha Beers, www.dancingfreedom.com

Guy Finley, The Life of Learning Foundation, www.guyfinley.com

Louise Diamond, Building a Culture of Peace, www.louisediamond.com

The Institute for Applied Spiritual Technology (IFAST) at Gita Nagari, www.gitanagari.com/

Diamond Mountain, founded by Geshe Michael Roach, www.diamondmtn.org

The Wise Woman Web and Susun Weed, www.wisewomanweb.com and www.susunweed.com

ALEPH: The Alliance for Jewish Renewal, www.aleph.org

Delphine Hano, www.emotionalserenity.com

Beth Rigby, Yoga Meets Dance, www.yogameetsdance.com

The Living Centre, www.thelivingcentre.com

The Global Peace Foundation, www.globalpeacefoundation.org

The World Peace Prayer Society, www.worldpeace.org

Living Oneness Foundation, www.livingonenessfoundation.com

The Living Essence Foundation, www.livingessence.com

Common Passion, www.commonpassion.org

The New Age Study of Humanity's Purpose, www.1spirit.com/eraofpeace/

A Tradition of Kindness, www.traditionofkindness.org

Partners in Kindness, www.partnersinkindness.org

Meditainment, www.meditainment.com

Brainwave with Todd, 6:00 to 8:00 a.m. Saturdays on KXCI Radio

The Intenders of the Highest Good, www.intenders.com

Earth Dance Multicultural Gatherings, www.earthdance8.org/

Be The Cause, www.BeTheCause.org

The Center for Spiritual Astrology, paulreeder.com

The EcoRebbe, Beyt Ohr Shekinah, Temple of the Light of the Divine Feminine Presence, home.earthlink.net/~ecorebbe

To Go Beyond, www.togobeyond.com

Divine Life Society, www.dlshq.org

Yeshivat Olam Echad: An Eco-Spiritual Alliance, www.yoe-lions.org

Soul Medicine Institute, Dawson Church, www.soulmedicineinstitute.org

Energy Psychology Press, www.energypsychologypress.com

Enlightened Professionals, www.eplic.org

Robert L. Nichol, StarDreams, www.stardreams-cropcircles.com

The Great Field, John James, PhD, www.thegreatfield.com

The Enchanted Garden: A History of Peace on Earth, www.lesliegoldman.com

Solar Healing, founded by H.R.M., solarhealing.com

SPEAK, Spiritual People Embracing Animals with Kindness, members.dodo.net.au/~kritters/

John Davies, www.cidcm.umd.edu/people/jdavies.htm

World Puja, www.worldpuja.org

AllOneNow, www.allonenow.org

Jeff Spiegel, home.utah.edu/~rfs4/jkm.htm

Ayman Sawaf-Sacred Commerce, www.AymanSawaf.com

We the Peoples, www.wethepeoples.org

Ananda Marga: Self-Realization and Service to Humanity, www.anandamarga.org

Circle of Lights, Bryan and Lisa James, www.circleoflights.com/

Barbara South: *Maybe You Should Think About This,* www.achieveradio.com/showpages/maybe.htm

The Academy for Future Science, Dr. J. J. Hurtak, www.affs.org

Warrior Arts, www.warriorarts.biz

Global Consciousness Project, noosphere.princeton.edu

Souled Out: Exploring Relationships from the Atom to the Infinite, www.souledout.org

Elite Books, Discovering Powerful New Ways of Relating. Publisher of *Healing the Heart of the World,* www.elitebooksonline.com

The One Reality, www.theonereality.com

The Tree of Life School, Joseph-Mark Cohen, www.treeoflifeschool.com

The Consciousness of the Christ: Reclaiming Jesus for a New Humanity, www.theconsciousnessofthechrist.com

The Happiness Club, www.happinessclub.com

Orlando Morales, www.orlandomorales.com

Experience Festival, www.experiencefestival.com

Way of the Corporate Shaman, Bill O'Mara, www.corporateshamanway.com

"Awaken," Martin Kettelhut, www.martinandsimon.com

Earth-Mountain View, www.earthmountainview.com

Great Dreams, www.greatdreams.com

Jah Levi, www.jahlevi.com

Michael Franti and Spearhead, www.spearheadvibrations.com

Joyce Shafer, www.lulu.com/content/127175

Southwest Interfaith Alliance, Sister Rebecca Therese, www.southwestinterfaith.org

ISKCON of Arizona, Dasarath and Sandamni

The Great Western Vehicle, Jhananda, www.greatwesternvehicle.org

Dr. Steven Hairfield, An American Monk, www.hairfield.com

The Conflict Resolution Center, www.drderi.com/

Toussaint L'Ouverture Charter High School for Arts and Social Justice,www.toussaintlouverture.org

Lilipoh Magazine of the Anthroposophical Society, www.lilipoh.com

Dhammaratanaran Temple University of Arizona Meditation Club, groups.yahoo.com/group/Meditation_Club/

Daniel R. Garcia, author of *The Sport of Distraction,* www.sportofdistraction.com

Peace Chain, www.peacechain.com

Lynn Sonntag, founding director, *Eco-Praxis;* research director, Sustainable Seattle

Vedic Meditation, www.introtomeditation.com

Sacred Peace Center, founded by Peace Mother Geeta Sacred Song, International Peace Shaman, www.sacredpeace.org

Mahamantra Das, president of Foundation for Religious Harmony and Universal Peace

Awakening of a Foot Soldier, Vets Meditating, www.awakeningofafootsolider.com

Sean G. Clarke, Peace Love Vision Musician, www.sgclarke.com

The Oracle Gatherings, www.oraclegatherings.com

The Digestive Wellness Center, www.digestivewellnesscenter.com

Union of Light, www.union-of-light.co.il

Love Flow, www.loveflow.us

Namaste Israel, www.namaste.co.il

Cafe Gratitude, www.withthecurrent.com

Riley Martin, www.rileymartin.tv

Cameron Burgess, www.cameronburgess.org

Meditation Society of Australia, www.meditation.org.au/

Hodaya, hodaya.co.il/default.aspx?PageId=7&NewsId=118

Zman Midbar, www.zmanmidbar.net

Culiut, www.culiut.com

Breathe for Peace, www.BreatheforPeace.org

Practice Yoga—Change the Planet, www.practicekindness.com

Real Peace, Peace Work in Israel, www.realpeace.org.il

Wake Up Laughing, with Swami Beyondananda,
www.wakeuplaughing.com

Point of Life, Michael Levy, www.pointoflife.com

Vaishali, www.PurpleV.com

The Universal Flag and Symbol, www.universalflag.org

Maryellen V. Little, The Power of Positive Thinking, GroupAime, and
Stephen McCrory, www.thebusinessmuse.com

GaiaField, www.gaiafield.net

Happy Oasis, www.happyoasis.com

Anodea Judith, www.WakingtheGlobalHeart.com

Self-Realization Fellowship, www.selfrealizationfellowship.org

God Bless Humanity, www.GodBlessHumanity.com

William Henry, www.williamhenry.net

Lynn McTaggart, the Intention Experiment,
www.theintentionexperiment.com

Teacher of Peace, www.TeacherOfPeace.org

Allarah's Holistic Alternatives, www.allarahsholisticalternatives.com

Asia Yoga Conference, www.AsiaYogaConference.com

Dr. David R. Hawkins, www.veritaspub.com

Dhama Boost, www.dboost.com

Young Jains of America and Dhrumil Purohit, www.yja.org

Jim Dreaver, www.jimdreaver.com/

Essence Training Institute, www.consciousevolution.org

The Desert Ashram, operated by Truth Consciousness (the legacy of Swami Amar Jyoti) {www.truthconsciousness.org}, joins in meditating daily, and regards the Peace Every Day Initiative as "worthy and lofty."

Joseph Giove, Stillpoint Center for Health Well-Being and Renewal, www.intendbalance.com

Frankie Lee Slater, www.circlesuniting.com, www.artofliving.com

Infinity Affinity, www.infinityaffinity.org

ACT ON WISDOM, P.O. Box 12484, Tucson, AZ 85732-2484, 206-335-6239 (voice), 734-661-7447 (fax), www.actonwisdom.com

Wise Awakening, www.wiseawakening.com

More all the time! Register at www.PeaceEveryDay.org

THE CULTURE OF LIFE COMMUNITY: GABRIELCOUSENS.COM

GABRIEL IS AVAILABLE ON HIS SOCIAL SPIRITUAL COLLABORA-
TIVE MEDIA NETWORK, gabrielcousens.com, in a variety of shows,
including *Alive with Gabriel,* and syndicated on media networks such as
wholelife.com. GabrielCousens.com is a social-spiritual media community of global citizens who value the Culture of Life and Liberation—
people who choose to live a healthy and ecological lifestyle that activates
the hologram of inner and outer world peace and liberation.

GabrielCousens.com is the next step in creating a virtual community
that supports all people in the transition to the Culture of Life, Peace, and
Liberation on every level. We invite you to join us—upload your profile,
share your creations in the sacred market, or upload your own video. We
look forward to your party-cipation!

Suggested Reading

Ambassadors of Peace: A Dialogue at the United Nations Between Dr. Robert Muller and Sant Darshan Singh. San José, Costa Rica: University for Peace, 1988.

Aron, Elaine, and Aron, Arthur. *The Maharishi Effect: A Revolution Through Meditation.* Walpole, N.H.: Stillpoint Publishing, 1986.

Baba, Meher. *Message by Meher Baba: The Religion of Life.* Seattle: W. C. Healy Press, 1945.

Beckwith, Michael Bernard. *40 Day Mind Fast Soul Feast.* DeVorss & Company, 2000.

Beckwith, Michael Bernard. *A Manifesto of Peace.* 2nd edition. Los Angeles: Agape Publishing, 2002.

Beckwith, Michael Bernard. *Inspirations of the Heart.* Los Angeles: Agape Publishing, 2004.

Blech, Benjamin, and Elaine Blech. *Your Name Is Your Blessing.* Jason Aronson, 1999.

Braden, Gregg. *The Isaiah Effect.* Three Rivers Press, 2001.

Braden, Gregg. *The God Code.* Hay House, 2005.

Braden, Gregg. *The Divine Matrix.* Hay House, 2006.

Braden, Gregg. *Secrets of the Lost Mode of Prayer.* Hay House, 2006.

Brown, Robert, and David Adelson. *The Maharishi Effect: Creating Coherence in World Consciousness: Promoting Positive and Evolutionary Trends Throughout the World: Results of Scientific Research 1974–1990.* Fairfield, Iowa: Maharishi Intl Univ Pr, 1990.

Carter, Vernon Gill, and Tom Dale. *Topsoil and Civilization.* Norman: University of Oklahoma Press, 1975.

Chandra, Harish. *Meat Eating: An Obstacle to Our Personal and Global Development.* Bangalore, India: Om Shantidhama, 2005.

Chandra, Harish. *The Human Nature and Human Food.* Hyderabad, India: Center for Inner Sciences, 2005.

Cousens, Gabriel. *Sevenfold Peace*. Tiburon, Calif.: H. J. Kramer, 1990.

Cousens, Gabriel. *Conscious Eating*. Revised edition. Berkeley: North Atlantic Books, 2000.

Cousens, Gabriel. *Depression-Free for Life*. Berkeley: HarperCollins, 2001.

Cousens, Gabriel. *Rainbow Green Live-Food Cuisine*. Berkeley: North Atlantic Books, 2003.

Cousens, Gabriel. *Spiritual Nutrition: Six Foundations for Spiritual Life and the Awakening of Kundalini*. Berkeley: North Atlantic Books, 2005.

Cousens, Gabriel. *There Is A Cure for Diabetes: The Tree of Life 21-Day Program*. Berkeley: North Atlantic Books, 2008.

Culi, Yaakov Rabbi. *The Torah Anthology*. New York: Maznaim Publishing Corporation, 1977.

de Mallac, Guy. *Gandhi's Seven Steps to Global Change*. Santa Fe: Ocean Tree Books, 1987.

Earth Works Group, The. *50 Simple Things You Can Do to Save the Earth*. Berkeley: Earthworks Press, 1989.

Edenite Society, The. *The Essene Humane Gospel of Jesus*. Santa Monica Society, 1978.

Eisenman, Robert. *James the Brother of Jesus*. New York: Penguin, 1998.

Eisenstein, Charles. *The Yoga of Eating*. Revised edition. NewTrends Publishing, 2003.

Eisler, Riane. *The Chalice and the Blade: Our History, Our Future*. New York: HarperOne, 1988.

Eisler, Riane. *The Real Wealth of Nations*. Berrett-Koehler Publishers, 2007.

Ewing, Upton Clary. *The Prophet of the Dead Sea Scrolls*. Revised edition. Progressive Press, 1994.

Falk, Harry. *Jesus the Pharisee: A New Look at the Jewishness of Jesus*. Wipf & Stock Publishers, 2003.

Federation of the Sufi Message, The. Toward the One: A Journal of Unity. www.sufimovement.org/pdf/TTO_2007.pdf

Ferencz, Benjamin B., and Ken Keyes, Jr. *Planethood: The Key to Your Survival and Prosperity*. Coos Bay, Ore.: Vision Books, 1993.

Friends of Peace Pilgrim. *Peace Pilgrim.* Santa Fe: Ocean Tree Books, 1982.

Gaster, Theodor H. *The Dead Sea Scriptures.* Anchor, 1986.

Gottlieb, Lynn. *She Who Dwells Within: A Feminist Vision of a Renewed Judaism.* HarperOne, 1995.

Greenpeace magazine, vol. 6, no. 6 (November-December 1988), and vol. 14, no. 1 (January-February 1989).

Hafiz, translated by Daniel Ladinzky. *The Gift.* Penguin, 1999.

Hanh, Thich Nhat. *Being Peace.* Second edition. Parallax Press, 2005.

Helminski, Edmund (translator). *The Ruins of the Heart: Selected Lyric Poetry of Jelaluddin Rumi.* Putney, Vt.: Threshold Books, 1981.

Herring, Basil. *Jewish Ethics and Halakha for Our Time,* Vol. 2. New York: Ktav Publishing, 1989.

Higa, Teruo. *An Earth Saving Revolution: A Means to Solve Our World's Problems through Effective Microorganisms,* Volumes I and II. First edition, EM America, 1993. Second edition, Sunmark Publishing, 1996.

Hubbard, Barbara Marx. *The Evolutionary Journey: A Personal Guide to a Positive Future.* San Francisco: Evolutionary Press, 1982. Distributed by Island Pacific Northwest.

Hurtak, J. J. *The Book of Knowledge: The Keys of Enoch.* Los Gatos: The Academy for Future Science. 1987. www.keysofenoch.org

Hurtak, J. J. "Commentary" in *The Molecule of Life.* Johannesburg, South Africa: SABC television documentary, 2001.

Hyland, J. R. *God's Covenant with Animals.* Lantern Books, 2000.

The Jerusalem Bible. Jerusalem: Koron Books, 2000.

Journal of the American Medical Association. "Diet and Stress in Vascular Disease." vol. 176, no. 9 (June 3, 1961).

Kaplan, Aryeh. *Meditation and Kabbalah.* Newburyport, Mass.: Weiser Books, 1989.

Knohl, Israel. *The Messiah Before Jesus.* Revised edition. Progressive Press, 1994.

Kook, Abraham Isaac. *Lights of Penitence, The Moral Principles, Lights of Holiness, Essays, Letters, and Poems.* New edition. Paulist Press, 1978.

Lamsa, George M. (translator). *Holy Bible from the Ancient Near Eastern Text.* HarperOne, 1985.

Lappé, Francis Moore. *Diet for a Small Planet.* 20th anniversary edition. Ballantine Books, 1991. www.smallplanet.org

Lappé, Francis Moore. *World Hunger: 12 Myths.* 2 Sub edition. Grove Press, 1998. www.smallplanet.org

Lappé, Francis Moore. *Getting a Grip: Clarity, Creativity, and Courage in a World Gone Mad.* Small Planet Media, 2007. www.smallplanet.org

Lappé, Francis Moore and Anna Lappé. *Hope's Edge: The Next Diet for a Small Planet.* Tarcher, 2002. www.smallplanet.org

Larson, Martin A. *The Story of Christian Origins,* Tahlequah, Okla.: Village Press, 1976.

Laurence, Richard (translator). *Book of Enoch: The Prophet.* Lushena Books, 2001.

Leloup, Jean-Yves. *The Gospel of Mary Magdalene.* Inner Traditions, 2002.

Lerner, Michael. *The Politics of Meaning: Restoring Hope and Possibility.* Addison-Wesley Publishing Company, 1997.

Lerner, Michael. *Spirit Matters.* Hampton Roads Publishing Company, 2002.

Lerner, Michael. *Healing Israel-Palestine: A Path to Peace and Reconciliation.* Berkeley: North Atlantic Books, 2003.

Mayer, Jean. *Dietary Goals for the U.S.* Cited by the U.S. Senate Select Committee on Nutrition and Human Needs. Washington, DC, February 1977.

McTaggart, Lynne. *The Field.* Harper Paperbacks, 2003.

Muhaiyaddeen, M. R. Bawa. *Come to the Secret Garden.* Philadelphia: The Fellowship Press, 1994.

Muhaiyaddeen, M. R. Bawa. *Islam and World Peace.* Philadelphia: The Fellowship Press, 2004.

Murti, Vasu. *They Shall Not Hurt or Destroy: Animal Rights and Vegetarianism in the Western Religious Traditions.* Cleveland: Vegetarian Advocates Press, 2003.

Nisbet, Robert. *History of the Idea of Progress.* New York: Basic Books, 1980.

Peace Pilgrim: Her Life and Work in Her Own Word. Santa Fe: Ocean Tree Books, 1994.

Pearse, Innes H., and Lucy H. Crocker. *The Peckham Experiment: A Study of the Living Structure of Society.* Rushden, Great Britain: Northamptonshire Printing and Publishing Co., 1947.

Phillips, R. "Coronary Heart Disease Mortality Among Seventh Day Adventists with Differing Dietary Habits." *The American Journal of Clinical Nutrition.* Abstract, American Public Health Association Meeting, Chicago, November 16–20, 1975.

Robbins, John. *Diet for a New America.* Walpole, N.H.: Stillpoint Publishing, 1987.

Russell, Peter. *The Global Brain: Speculations on the Evolutionary Leap to Planetary Consciousness.* Los Angeles: J. P. Tarcher, 1983.

Savedow, Steve. *Sepher Rezial Hemelach: The Book of the Angel Rezial.* Weiser Books, 2000.

Sawaf, Ayman, and Rowan Gabrielle. *Sacred Commerce: The Rise of the Global Citizen.* Mill Valley, Calif.: Sacred Commerce, 2007.

Schiffman, Lawrence H. *Reclaiming the Dead Sea Scrolls.* Anchor, 1995.

Schonefield, Hugh. *The Essene Odyssey.* New edition. Element Books, 1993.

Schwartz, Richard H. *Judaism and Vegetarianism.* Marblehead, Mass.: Micah Publications, 1988.

Sears, David. *The Vision of Eden: Animal Welfare and Vegetarianism in Jewish Law and Mysticism.* Orot, 2003.

St. Augustine. *The Confessions.* Washington, DC: Catholic University Press, 1953.

Stolper, Pinchas. *The Aryeh Kaplan Anthology I and II.* Noble Book Press Corp., 2004.

Szekely, Edmond Bordeaux. *The Gospel of the Essenes.* The C. W. Daniel Co., Ltd., 1974.

Szekeley, Edmond Bordeaux. *The Essene Jesus.* Nelson, B.C.: International Biogenic Society,1977.

Szekely, Edmond Bordeaux. *The Essene Code of Life*. Nelson, B.C.: International Biogenic Society, 1978.

Szekely, Edmond Bordeaux. *The Essene Origins of Christianity*. Nelson, B.C.: International Biogenic Society, 1980.

Szekely, Edmond Bordeaux. *The Discovery of the Essene Gospel of Peace*. Nelson, B.C.: International Biogenic Society, 1981.

Szekely, Edmond Bordeaux. *The Essene Gospel of Peace, Book 1: The Unknown Books of the Essenes*. Nelson, B.C.: International Biogenic Society, 1981.

Szekely, Edmond Bordeaux. *The Essene Gospel of Peace, Book 2: The Unknown Books of the Essenes*. Nelson, B.C.: International Biogenic Society, 1981.

Szekely, Edmond Bordeaux. *The Essene Gospel of Peace, Book 3: Lost Scrolls of the Essene Brotherhood*. Nelson, B.C.: International Biogenic Society, 1981.

Szekely, Edmond Bordeaux. *The Essene Gospel of Peace, Book 4: The Teachings of the Elect*. Nelson, B.C.: International Biogenic Society, 1981.

Szekely, Edmond Bordeaux. *The Essene Science of Fasting and the Art of Sobriety*. Nelson, B.C.: International Biogenic Society, 1981.

Szekely, Edmond Bordeaux. *The Essene Way: Biogenic Living*. Nelson, B.C.: International Biogenic Society, 1981.

Szekely, Edmond Bordeaux. *The Essenes by Josephus and His Contemporaries*. Nelson, B.C.: International Biogenic Society, 1981.

Szekely, Edmond Bordeaux. *The Essene Science of Life*. Nelson, B.C.: International Biogenic Society, 1985.

Szekely, Edmond Bordeaux. *From Enoch to the Dead Sea Scrolls*. Nelson, B.C.: International Biogenic Society, 1981.

Tuttle, Will. *The World Peace Diet*. Lantern Books, 2005.

Twyman, James F. *Portrait of the Master*. Findhorn Press, 2000.

Twyman, James F. *The Secret of the Beloved Disciple*. Findhorn Press, 2000.

Twyman, James F. *Ten Spiritual Lessons I Learned At the Mall*. Findhorn Press, 2001.

Twyman, James F. *Emissary of Love: The Psychic Children Speak to the World.* Hampton Roads Publishing Co., 2002.

Twyman, James F. *The Prayer of St. Francis.* Findhorn Press, 2002.

Twyman, James F. *A Proposing Tree.* Hampton Roads Publishing Co., 2003.

Twyman, James F. *The Art of Spiritual Peacemaking: Secret Teachings from Jeshua ben Joseph.* Findhorn Press, 2006.

Twyman, James F. *Emissary of Light.* Findhorn Press, 2007.

Twyman, James F. *The Moses Code: The Most Powerful Manifestation Tool in the History of the World.* Hay House, 2008.

Twyman, James F., and Diana Cooper. *Angel Inspiration: Together, Humans and Angels Have the Power to Change the World.* 2007.

Vaclavik, Charles P. *The Vegetarianism of Jesus Christ.* Three Rivers, Calif.: Kaweah Publishing Co., 1986.

Vanderkam, James C. *The Dead Sea Scrolls Today.* SPCK Publishing, 1994.

Vaughan, Frances, and Roger Walsh (eds.). *A Gift of Peace: Selections from a Course in Miracles.* New York: St. Martin's Press, 1986.

Vegetarian Times, Issue 152 (April 1990). Published by Vegetarian Life and Times, Inc. (Illinois).

Weitzman, Gideon. *Sparks of Light.* Jason Aronson, 1999.

Wilson, Edmund. *Israel and the Dead Sea Scrolls.* Moyer Bell, 2000.

Wise, Elia. *A Letter to Earth.* Harmony Books, 2000.

Zajic, Lenka Jane. "Living Examples Survey: An Investigation of People Who Have Eaten a Raw Foods Diet for Over Two Years." Thesis for Vegan Live-Food Spiritual Nutrition Master's Program offered by the Tree of Life Foundation through the University of Integrated Science, 2006.

Resources

ECOLOGY

Agricultural Carbon Sequestering
www.montana.edu/wwwpb/pubs/
mt200313.html

Anaerobic digestion
en.wikipedia.org/wiki/Anaerobic_
digestion
Norway's Use of Anaerobic
digestion for its power, and
teaching prison inmates
permaculture for food self-
sufficiency (as reported by Michael
Moore in *Sicko*).

Blue Planet Project
blueplanetproject.org

Center for Marine Conservation
1725 DeSales St. NW
Washington, DC 20036

**Citizens' Clearinghouse for
Hazardous Waste**
P.O. Box 926
Arlington, VA 22216

Citizens for a Better Environment
33 East Congress, Suite 523
Chicago, IL 60605

Citizens for a Better Environment
942 Market St., Suite 505
San Francisco, CA 94102

Conservation International
1015 18th St. NW
Washington, DC 20036

The Cornucopia Foundation
www.Cornucopia.org

Die Verbraucher Initiative
Koinstr 198
Postfach 17 46
5300 Bonn I, West Germany
(02 28) 65 90 44

**Earth Garden Project Transculture,
Inc.**
496 Hudson St. #826
New York, NY 10014

Earthjustice
426 17th Street, 6th Floor
Oakland, CA 94612-2820
(510) 550-6700
earthjustice.org

Earth Island Institute
300 Broadway, Suite 28
San Francisco, CA 94133

EarthSave
315 Quail Terrace
Ben Lomond, CA 95005
(408) 423-4069

Empowerment Institute
www.empowermentinstitute.net

Environmental Defense Fund
1616 P St. NW, Suite 150
Washington, DC 20036

Environmental Policy Institute
218 D St.
Washington, DC 20003
(202) 544-2600

Ethiquette
www.ethiquette.ca/

Food First, Institute for Food and Development Policy
www.Food-first.org
With "Campesino a Campesino:
Voices from Latin America's Farmer
to Farmer Movement for
Sustainable Agriculture."

Friends of the Earth
530 7th St. SE
Washington, DC 20003
(202) 543-4312

GreenHome
www.greenhome.com
Environmental commerce to green
your home

Greenhouse Crisis Foundation
1130 17th St. NW, Suite 630
Washington, DC 20036

Greenpeace, USA Headquarters
1436 U St. NW
Washington, DC 20009
(202) 462-1177

Green Program Project
P.O. Box 111
Burlington, VT 05402

Green Society
www.greensociety.org

International Union for Conservation of Nature and Natural Resources
Gland 1196, Switzerland

International Wildlife Coalition
1807 H St. NW, Suite 301
Washington, DC 20006
(202) 347-0822

Japan Public Citizen
9th Floor, Central Building
1-1-5 Kyobashi, Chuo-Ku
Tokyo, 104, Japan
(03) 272-3900

Local Harvest
www.LocalHarvest.org

National Audubon Society
645 Pennsylvania Ave. SE
Washington, DC 20003

National Wildlife Federation
1412 16th St. NW
Washington, DC 20036

Natural Resources Defense Council
40 West 20th St.
New York, NY 10011

Nature Conservancy International
1800 North Kent St., Suite 800
Arlington, VA 22209
www.nature-conservancy.org

New Forests Fund
731 Eighth St.
Washington, DC 20003

New Zealand Nuclear Free Zone
Committee
Box 18541
Christchurch 9 New Zealand
889-816

Nuclear Awareness Project
730 Bathhurst St.
Toronto, Ontario, Canada M5S 2R4
(416) 537-0438

Oceanic Society
218 D St. SE
Washington, DC 20003

Permaculture for Urban Sewage
Treatment
www.environ-
mentalproductions.com/ecoparque

Rainforest Action Network
300 Broadway, Suite 28
San Francisco, CA 94133

Remineralize the Earth
www.remineralize.org
Giving back to the Earth through
rebuilding a high-mineral topsoil is
an integral and essential way of
being peace and creating peace.

Renew America
1001 Connecticut Ave. NW,
Suite 1719
Washington, DC 20036

Rocky Mountain Institute
1739 Snowmass Creek Rd.
Snowmass, CO 81654

Sane Freeze
711 G Street
Washington, DC 20002

Sierra Club
P.O. Box 7603
San Francisco, CA 94120-9826
(415) 776-2211

The Small Planet Institute
25 Mt. Auburn St., Suite 203
Cambridge, MA 02138
(617) 441-6300, x115
Fax: (617) 441-6307
www.smallplanet.org

SunEnergy
P.O. Box 8371 Symonds
Auckland, New Zealand

David Suzuki Foundation
www.davidsuzuki.org

Todd Ecological Society for
Development of "Living Machines"
www.toddecological.com

Tree of Life Foundation
Attn: Spiritual Veganic Farming
Program
PO Box 778
Patagonia, AZ 85624
(520) 394-2520
www.treeoflife.nu

Water Aid
wateraid.org

Wilderness Society
1400 I St. NW, 10th floor
Washington, DC 20005

World Resources Institute
1735 New York Ave. NW
Washington, DC 20006

Worldwatch Institute
1776 Massachusetts Ave. NW
Washington, DC 20036

World Wildlife Fund
1250 24th St. NW, 5th floor
Washington, DC 20037

Zero Waste
www.zerowaste.org

HEALTH

American Vegan Society
501 Old Harding Highway
Malaga, NJ 08328

Center for Science in the Public Interest, Americans for Safe Food
1501 16th St. NW
Washington, DC 20036
(202) 332-9110

Citizens Concerned About Food Irradiation
Box 236, Red Hill
Queensland, Australia 4059

Dances of Liberation
www.parashakti.org

First Christians Essene Church
2536 Collier Ave.
San Diego, CA 92116

Food and Water, Inc.
225 Lafayette #612
New York, NY 10012
(212) 941-9340

Food First
1885 Mission St.
San Francisco, CA 94103
(415) 864-8555

Foundation Soleil
Bois des Arts 38
CH 1225 Geneva, Switzerland
022 489676

Golden Bridge Yoga
www.goldenbridgeyoga.com

Hippocrates Health Institute
www.hippocratesinst.org

International Bioenergetic Society (IBS)
Box 205
Matsqui, British Columbia, Canada
VOX IS0

International Organization of Consumer Unions (IOCU)
Box 1045
10830 Penang, Malaysia
(604) 371-396

Jivamukti Yoga
www.jivamuktiyoga.com

Living Machines Water and Ecological Systems
www.livingmachines.com

London Food Commission
Box 291
London, N51DU, United Kingdom
(01) 633-578

Meetup Groups
www.meetup.com
Search for keywords and phrases such as raw food, meditation, organic farming, or inner peace, and enter your zip code. Meetup groups for such topics exist in many cities and towns.

Mercola Health News
www.Mercola.com

The Moving Centers
www.GabrielleRoth.com

National Coalition to Stop Food Irradiation
P.O. Box 59-0488
San Francisco, CA 94159
(415) 626-2734

Naturally Occurring Standards Group (NOSG)
6771 S. Silver Hill Drive, Finland, MN 55603
(218) 226 4164
Email: info@nosg.org
www.nosg.org

North American Vegetarian Society
P.O. Box 72
Dolgeville, NY 13329

Open International University for Complementary Medicines
Chair of Energy Medicine: Dr. Sandra Rose Michael
www.oiucm.org

Spiritual Emergence Network Institute of Transpersonal Psychology
250 Oak Grove Ave.
Menlo Park, CA 94025
(415) 327-2776

Tree of Life Rejuvenation Center
Attn: Rejuvenation, Detoxification, and Whole Person Healing Programs
PO Box 778
Patagonia, AZ 85624

(520) 394-2520
www.treeoflife.nu

Viva! Vegetarians International Voice for Animals
www.Viva.org.uk

World Organization of Natural Medicine
www.wonm.org

World Research Foundation
15300 Ventura Blvd., Suite 405
Sherman Oaks, CA 91403
(818) 907-5483

THOUGHT FORMS FOR PEACE

Agape International Spiritual Centers
www.agapelive.org
Culver City, CA

B'nei Baruch Kabbalah Education and Research Institute
www.kabbalah.info

Conscious Humanity
www.conscioushumanity.com

Essene organizations:
www.EsseneWay.org
Essenes.net
Essenes.org
Essene.org
Essene.com

Group Avatar
P.O. Box 4155
Tucson, AZ 85738

The Kabbalah Centre
www.kabbalah.com

Karuna Foundation
P.O. Box 11422
Berkeley, CA 94701

Monadnock Mindfulness Practice
www.mindfulness.us
103 Roxbury St., Suite 301
Keene, NH

The Noon Fellowship
Box 110
Weston, Ontario, Canada M9N
3M6

Operation Planet Love
Calle Adolfo Prieto No. 125-D-501
Col. Del Valle C.P. 03100
Mexico, DF, Mexico

Peace Every Day Initiative
www.peaceeveryday.org

Peace the 21st
1474 Bathhurst St.
Toronto, Ontario, Canada M5P 3G9
(416) 541-5477
Fax: (416) 651-8831

Peace the 21st, Sonoma County
Martina Hill
(707) 632-5627
martinahill7@comcast.net

Pentagon Meditation Club
105 Overlook Dr.
Cross Junction, VA 22625
(540) 888-4960
Fax: (540) 333-4961
www.pentagonmeditationclub.org
www.peacemakersinstitute.org

People for Planetary Peace
845 Via de la Paz
Pacific Palisades, CA 90272
One hour a month for peace on the
last day of each month.

Positive Thinking Planetary Network
Anse St. Jean
Quebec, Canada GOV IJO
Love chain, fifteen minutes each
Sunday at 12:00 noon local time.

Quartus Foundation
P.O. Box 1768
Boerne, TX 78006-6768
(512) 328-0673

Shekum Foundation
5968 Chabot Crest
Oakland, CA 94618
(415) 547-4230

The Society of Prayer for World Peace
800 3rd Ave., 31st floor
New York, NY 10022
(212) 755-4755

Swedenborgian Community
swedenborgiancommunity.org

Tree of Life Foundation
PO Box 778
Patagonia, AZ 85624
(520) 394-2520
www.treeoflife.nu

PEACE WITH THE BODY

Lifeforce
www.lifeforcefoundation.org

Life Force Arts Foundation
www.lifeforcearts.org

Visions Life Force Foundation
www.viisionslifeforcefoundation.
com

Peace with the Mind

Academy for Future Sciences
affs@affs.org
www.affs.org
P.O. Box FE, Los Gatos, CA 95031,
USA
P.O. Box 35340, Menlo Park, 0102,
Pretoria, South Africa

Emotional Literacy Campaign
www.feel.org

Emotional Literacy Education
www.emotionalliteracyeducation.
com

Institute of Noetic Sciences (IONS)
www.noetic.org
IONS supports leading-edge
research into the potentials and
powers of the consciousness—
perceptions, beliefs, attention,
intention, and intuition. The
institute explores phenomena that
do not necessarily fit conventional
scientific models, while
maintaining a commitment to
scientific rigor.

The Intuition Network
Kevin Ryerson
www.Intution.org

Joy of Life Organization
www.joyoflife.com

Life of Learning Foundation
www.lifeoflearning.org

Tree of Life Rejuvenation Center
Attn: Zero Point Process
PO Box 778
Patagonia, AZ 85624
(520) 394-2520
www.treeoflife.nu

University of Peace
Costa Rica
www.upeace.org

Peace with the Family

Partnership Way
www.PartnershipWay.org
Riane Eisler

Tree of Life Rejuvenation Center
Attn: Sacred Relationships
PO Box 778
Patagonia, AZ 85624
(520) 394-2520
www.treeoflife.nu

Peace with Community

Action Linkage
5828 Telegraph
Oakland, CA 94609

Act on Wisdom
P.O. Box 12484
Tucson, AZ 85732-2484
(206) 335-6239
Fax: (734) 661-7447
www.actonwisdom.com

African Link
P.O. Box 72723
Ndola, Zambia

American Friends Service Committee
1501 Cherry St.
Philadelphia, PA 19102
(215) 241-7000

American Society for the Prevention of Cruelty to Animals
441 East 92nd St.
New York, NY 10128
(212) 876-7700

A New American Place
283 Marina Blvd.
San Francisco, CA 94123

Animal Rights International
Box 214
Planetarium Station
New York, NY 10024

Auroville
www.auroville.org
A universal city in the making in south India

Better World Society
1140 Connecticut
Washington, DC 20036

Beyond War
222 High St.
Palo Alto, CA 94301
(415) 851-2626

The Big ONE
www.beautifulcommunities.org
The Bristol Group
13, The Drive

Henlease, Bristol, BS9, United Kingdom

Center for Peace
880 Graves-Delozier Road
Seymour, TN 37865-7012
(865) 428-3070
Fax: (865) 429-0842
www.centerforpeace.us

Center for Soviet-American Dialogue
14426 N.E. 16th Pl.
Bellevue, WA 98003

Center for Sustainable Development
P.O. Box 120
Ipswich, MA 01938
(508) 768-6742

Centre Link Trust
31 Grove End Rd.
London, NW8 9LY, United Kingdom

Centro de Amigos Para la Paz
50 M. Este OLJ
San Jose, Costa Rica
(506) 51-38-49

Children as Peacemakers
950 Battery St.
San Francisco, CA 94111
(415) 981-0916

Christic Institute
1324 North Capitol St. NW
Washington, DC 20002
(202) 797-8106

Clean Water Action Project
317 Pennsylvania Ave.
Washington, DC 20003

Common Cause
2030 M St. NW
Washington, DC 20036

Doves of Peace
3 Lendon Place
Macgregor, Australia

Earth First!
P.O. Box 5871
Tucson, AZ 85703

Earthlight
1226 Jenifer
Madison, WI 53703

EarthLink
P.O. Thora
N.S.W. 2454 Australia

EarthNet
225 Kahoea Pl.
Kula, Maui, HI 96790
(808) 878-2024

Earth Stewards
6330 Eagle Harbor Dr.
Bainbridge Island, WA 98136

Encounter Point
EncounterPoint.com

Findhorn One-Earth Network
The Park
Forres, IV36 OTZ, Scotland

Fraternidad Universal
P.O. Box 943
Geheregia, Costa Rica 37-2019

Friends of Animals, Inc.
11 West 60th St.
New York, NY 10023
(212) 247-8077

The Fund for Animals
200 W. 57th St.
New York, NY 10019
(212) 246-2096

Gaiafield
www.Gaiafield.net

Global Citizen
11886 Oaude Court
Northglenn, CO 80233
(303) 457-2465

Global Family
112 Jordan Ave.
San Anselmo, CA 94960
(415) 453-7600

Global Security Institute
www.gsinstitute.org

Grassroots International
P.O. Box 312
Cambridge, MA 02139
(617) 497-9180

Green Net
26028 Underwood STR
London, Nl 7JQ, United Kingdom

Humanity Unites Brilliance
www.hubhub.org

Infinity Affinity
www.infinityaffinity.org

Institute for Planetary Synthesis
P.O. Box 128
CH-1211 Geneva 20 Switzerland

Institute of Noetic Science
475 Gate Five Road
Sausalito, CA 94965
(415) 331-5650

International Network for U.N. Second Assembly
308 Cricklewood Lane
London, NW2 2PX, United Kingdom

International Society for Animal Rights, Inc.
421 South State St.
Clarks Summit, PA 18411
(717) 586-2200

National Anti-Vivisection Society
100 East Ohio St.
Chicago, IL 60611
(312) 787-4486

Ojai Foundation
P.O. Box 1620
Ojai, CA 93023

One Society
2616 Iron St.
Bellingham, WA 98225
(206) 676-4408

Our Planet in Every Classroom
21 Inglewood Drive
Toronto, Ontario, Canada M4T IG7
(416) 485-6221

Peace Child
3977 Chain Bridge
Fairfax, VA 22030

The Peace Curriculum, Inc.
1014 20th Ave., SE
Minneapolis, MN 55414
(612) 623-8012

PeaceInsight
www.peaceinsight.org
A peace education organization for teenagers from Palestine and Israel

Peace Is Possible
2008 Grand Ave. S
Minneapolis, MN 55405

Peace Links
747 8th St. SE
Washington, DC 20003

Peacemakers, Inc.
P.O. Box 141254
Dallas, TX 75214
(214) 871-8448

The Peace Pole Project
P.O. Box 170279
San Francisco, CA 94117
(415) 731-7917
Fax: (415) 731-7923

Peace Through Understanding
P.O. Box 95910
2509 CX, The Hague, The Netherlands

Pentagon Meditation Club
105 Overlook Dr.
Cross Junction, VA 22625
(540) 888-4960
Fax: (540) 888-4961
www.pentagonmeditationclub.org

People for the Ethical Treatment of Animals (PETA)
P.O. Box 42516
Washington, DC 20015
(202) 726-0156

Physicians for Social Responsibility
1601 Connecticut Ave.
Washington, DC 20009

Planetary Citizens
P.O. Box 1045
Mt. Shasta, CA 96067

Public Citizen (Ralph Nader)
2000 P St. NW #605
Washington, DC 20036

Radio Peace
P.O. Box 1143
Arleta, CA 91331

The Raoul Wallenberg Institute
www.raoulwallenberginstitute.org

Reutsadaka
www.reutsadaka.org
Arab-Jewish youth partnership

Rotary Peace
1560 Sherman Ave.
Evanston, IL 60201

SacredCommerce
www.sacredcommerce.com

SEVA Foundation
8 N. San Pedro Rd.
San Rafael, CA 94903
(415) 492-1829
www.seva.org

Spirit of Circles Uniting
Frankie Lee Slater
www.artofliving.com and
www.circlesuniting.com

Traubman Family
traubman.igc.org
Building a Jewish community

Tree of Life Foundation
Attn: Working and Living at the
Tree of Life
PO Box 778
Patagonia, AZ 85624
(520) 394-2520
www.treeoflife.nu

United Nations Environmental Program
United Nations Plaza
New York, NY 10017

The University for Peace
Apartado 95 Barrio
San Jose, 1005 Costa Rica 34-10-48

Vessels of Peace
www.vesselsofpeace.com

The Victoria Trust
P.O. Box 1023
2240AB Wassenaar, Holland

Whole Earth Satellite Network
13445 Ventura Blvd.
Sherman Oaks, CA 91413
(818) 829-4736

WholeLife
www.wholelife.com

World Peace Center
P.O. Box 95062
Lincoln, NE 68509
(402) 477-4733

Year of Love
www.yearoflove.org

PEACE WITH CULTURE

Arizona Project for Spirituality
Arizona State University School of
Social Work
ssw.asu.edu/spirituality/azpssw/
index.html

Buffalo Messenger
www.BuffaloMessengers.com

The Celestine Vision
James and Salle Redfield
www.celestinevision.org

Creativity For Peace
www.creativityforpeace.com
A year-round program that brings
adolescent girls from Palestine and
Israel out of the violence into the
safe countryside for a summer
program that teaches leadership
and communication skills and
promotes understanding, trust, and
reconciliation

Foundation for Conscious Evolution
Barbara Marx Hubbard
www.evolve.org
Pioneering in positive options for
the future of humanity for forty
years

Foundation for the Law of Time
www.lawoftime.org

Friendship for Universal Peace
www.shelfari.com/groups/12965/
about

Global Art Project
www.global-art.org

GlobeSonic
www.GlobeSonic.com
International music organization
involved in the production of
groundbreaking tours, shows, and
festivals

Healing Sounds
www.healingsounds.com

**Indigenous Support Group
Association**
Contact: Alberto Romero
(520) 313-5624
spiritdance@treeoflife.nu
Humanity in Unity
www.HumanityinUnity.org

**International Center on Nonviolent
Conflict**
www.Nonviolent-Conflict.org
(202) 416-4720
Fax: (202) 466-5918
icnc@nonviolent-conflict.org

Jerusalem Peacemakers
www.jerusalem-peacemakers.org

**LULAC, League of United Latin
American Countries**
www.lulac.org

Macrocosm USA
Possibilities for a New Progressive
Era
www.macronet.org/
brockway@macronet.org
P.O. Box 185
Cambria, CA 93428
(805) 927-2515

Marin Sufis
www.marinsufis.org

New Group of World Servers
www.ngws.org

Pathways to Peace (PTP)
Avon Mattison, founder
www.pathwaystopeace.org
An international peace building, education, and consulting organization

The Peace Alliance
www.thepeacealliance.org
Campaign to establish a U.S. Department of Peace and the Peace Alliance Foundation

Planet Art Network
www.planetartnetwork.info/

Planet Coexist
www.planetcoexist.com

Steve Robertson
Founder/executive producer, Project-Peace on Earth; campaign founder, Peace Has Begun
www.project-peaceonearth.org

Salaam Shalom Radio—Muslims and Jews Talking Together
www.salaamshalom.org.uk/

Shaikh Abdul Aziz Bohari and the Sons of Abraham
www.jerusalem-academy.org

Sufi Circle
www.suficircle.com

Sufi Sheikh Ghassan from Nazareth
www.nswas.org/

Sulha Peace Project
www.Sulha.com

Tamir: Combining Poetry with Movement
www.rumi-wayoftheheart.com

Tikkun Community and Network of Spiritual Progressives
www.Tikkun.org

Tree of Life Rejuvenation Center
Attn: Cultural and Music Performances and Retreats
PO Box 778
Patagonia, AZ 85624
(520) 394-2520
www.treeoflife.nu

Urth.tv
www.urth.tv

White Buffalo Sanctuary Foundation
Little Golden Bear Cynthia Hart
www.cynthiahart.com

PEACE WITH GOD

Modern Seers
www.modernseers.org

Sufi University
www.sufiuniversity.org

ECONOMICS

Campesino a Campesino
www.viacampesina.org and
www.foodfirst.org

Co-op America and various Green Business networks and associations
www.coopamerica.org

EcoGift Association
www.EcoGift.com

Local Harvest
www.localharvest.org

Sacred Commerce
sacredcommerce.com
www.urth.tv/content/
blogcate-gory/184/246/

About the Author

REBBE GABRIEL COUSENS, MD, MD(H), Diplomat American Board of Holistic Medicine, and Diplomat in Ayurveda, is the founder and director of the Tree of Life Foundation and Tree of Life Rejuvenation Center in Patagonia, Arizona, and Tree of Light Foundation and Tree of Life by the Dead Sea. He is married to Shanti GoldsCousens and has two children, Heather and Rafael, and two grandchildren, Rhea and Katja.

Dr. Cousens serves as a holistic medical doctor, a licensed psychiatrist and family therapist, a licensed homeopathic physician in the state of Arizona, and as a Rebbe who functions as a physician of the soul. He uses the modalities of nutrition, naturopathy, Ayurveda, homeopathy, and transpersonal psychotherapy blended with spiritual awareness in the healing of body, mind, and spirit. He is the successful author of numerous books including *Spiritual Nutrition, Conscious Eating, Rainbow Green Live-Food Cuisine, Sevenfold Path of Peace, Depression-Free for Life, Tachyon Energy: A New Paradigm in Holistic Healing,* co-authored with David Wagner, and *There Is A Cure for Diabetes,* his most recent. Dr. Cousens has been the host of the radio programs *Physician of the Soul* and *Creating Peace by Being Peace,* and he facilitates the spiritual, nutritional, and lifestyle support tele-seminars "Alive With Gabriel." He is recognized as an international peaceworker and spiritual teacher, and creator of transformative programs at the Tree of Life, including the highly effective 21-Day Program for Healing Diabetes Naturally at the Tree of Life Rejuvenation Center in the U.S. and Tree of Life by the Dead Sea. He is also recognized as the world's leading medical authority on live-food nutrition.

Rebbe Cousens, a certified Senior Essene teacher since 1988, founded the Essene Order of Light in 1992. He received a pastoral rabbinical initiation from Rabbi Gershon Winkler in 2001 and serves as a spiritual teacher of the living Jewish-Essene way, including teaching and guiding the whole cycle of Jewish holidays at the Tree of Life, leading weekly

Kabbalat Shabbats at the Tree of Life U.S. and in Israel when on site, and leading Kabbalat Shabbats in Europe, Greece, and Meso-America. Dr. Cousens has presented seminars on many topics including health and nutrition, psycho-spiritual healing, and spiritual awareness throughout the United States, Canada, Europe, Israel, Mexico, Costa Rica, India, Egypt, Lebanon, Morocco, Bali, and Hong Kong. He is a frequent guest on popular radio talk shows, including the radio show *Across America,* and has been a health and nutrition columnist. Dr. Cousens has published numerous articles in health journals and popular magazines in the areas of biochemistry, school health, clinical pharmacology, hypoglycemia, and Alzheimer's disease.

As part of his multi-cultural life and spiritual training, Rebbe Cousens spent seven years under the tutelage of Swami Muktananda Paramahansa and eleven years with Swami Prakashananda Saraswati. In 1981 he was empowered to give Shaktipat by Swami Muktananda. Since 1976 he has been teaching meditation. As part of his interfaith spiritual background, he has also studied in the Sufi tradition of Murshid Samuel Lewis. A four-year sundancer in the Lakota tradition who was adopted into the High Horse clan and appointed leader of the Yellow Horse Clan, he has started annual One World Spirit Dances for peace in both Arizona and Israel.

Rebbe Cousens is a spiritual teacher who speaks from direct experience prior to the I Am awareness. His teachings of the Sevenfold Path of Peace, Six Foundations for Spiritual Life, and the awakening of Kundalini create the conditions for experiencing the divine bliss that is the primary motivation for liberation as it achieves the urge to live in an unending Divine Kiss. His deep personal experience in the Jewish, Essene, Kabbalist, Native American, Yogic, and Sufi traditions have allowed him to penetrate to the essence of spiritual life in a way that transcends the ego and ethnocentric perceptions that have become such a source of conflict and confusion in the world. This deep, wide, and unusual background gives Rebbe Cousens a unique ability to provide spiritual, humanitarian interfaith insight and peace work in culturally diverse situations.

A cum laude graduate of Amherst College, where he was captain of an undefeated football team, Dr. Cousens was selected as an All New England guard and middle linebacker and one of eleven National Scholar Athletes inducted into the National Football Hall of Fame. He received his MD degree from Columbia Medical School in 1969 and completed his psychiatric residency in 1973.

A former member of the Board of Trustees of the American Holistic Medical Association, he is listed in *Who's Who in California*, *Who's Who Among Top Executives*, *Who's Who in Executives and Professionals*, *the International Who's Who of Entrepreneurs*, and *Strathmore's Who's Who*.

Since 1965 Dr. Cousens has been involved in humanitarian projects, including working with African American teen gangs in Southside Chicago for several years in the mid-sixties. In his second year in medical school, as head of the regional Student Health Organization, he organized doctors and medical students from nine different medical schools in the region to set up an evening clinic at PS 175, a grammar school located one block from Harlem Hospital. They examined more than 500 children in one week, and after analyzing the results, Dr. Cousens developed a training program for community mothers, with funding from the U.S. Department of Health, Education, and Welfare. This program was so successful that it spread to more than half the schools in Central Harlem. By the time he graduated from Columbia, the program had been adopted and financed by the New York Department of Health. While in New York, Dr. Cousens also developed a sickle-cell screening program at PS 175. The results of this program were also followed through by the New York Department of Health.

After graduating from medical school, Dr. Cousens received an appointment at the National Institute of Mental Health in community psychiatry. He also received a commission as lieutenant commander in the Public

Health Service where he served for three years. During his medical internship, he developed several community programs in San Francisco supporting socio-cultural peace. When he moved to Boston for his psychiatric residency, Dr. Cousens developed a teen center for white, working-class teenagers providing family therapy and teen counseling as well as social activities. In 1973 he moved to Petaluma, California, where he became a consultant for the California State Department of Mental Health. He also became the chief mental health consultant for Sonoma County Head Start programs, which ranged over an area of almost 300 miles. During this time, he worked with white, working-class parents and Pomo Native American parents and teachers to develop a Head Start program that included teaching family dynamics to Head Start teachers and developing an innovative lead-screening program. Over a period of several years, Dr. Cousens established the Petaluma People's Services Center, a community-based network that provides a comprehensive range of social services for all of Sonoma County as well as enhanced networking communication with over forty agencies. This center is still operating successfully twenty-five years later and has become a significant social service agency in southern Sonoma County.

Currently, the focus of Dr. Cousens's humanitarian work is creating world peace on all levels. He has been leading peace meditations around the world since 1985 including Peace 21 meditations where people come together at one time to meditate for peace four times a year on each equinox and solstice. In 1996, he established this quarterly peace meditation at the United Nations in New York for world peace. This is all part of an overall process to create peace and healing of the planet on the physical, mental, and spiritual levels. In 2003, he initiated the worldwide Peace Every Day Initiative to encourage all traditions to meditate collectively for peace. The Dalai Lama has given his blessings to the project.

In 2007 Dr. Cousens launched the 21-Day Program for Healing Diabetes Naturally Program at the Tree of Life centers in both the U.S. and Israel. This program, which has up to 90 percent success in healing

Type-2 diabetes, is being slowly introduced to the Native American population. He is also working with the League of Latin American Communities (LULAC) to introduce the program in the U.S to the Latino communities in Mexico, Central America, and South America. At the July 1999 Native American Sundance, Dr. Cousens had a vision of the possibility of feeding the hungry children of the world. Using technologies that are being incorporated at the Tree of Life Foundation, such as EM (Effective Microorganisms), low-water growing, and dilute salt-water technologies, agriculture production can be increased two to ten times over and facilitate the conversion from commercial to organic-quality and high-production food in one year. Presently, Dr. Cousens is working in cooperation with the Panamanian government to establish these eco-health, education-agricultural villages for the disadvantaged peoples.

Rebbe Cousens's peace and spiritual commitment have taken him to Israel where he has become a popular teacher and has established the Tree of Life at the Dead Sea (ten minutes from the ancient Essene settlement in Qumran). Part of his humanitarian mission is to support the peace process in the Middle East. Rebbe Cousens has committed his life to world service and to establishing these programs on an international basis so that he, and everyone who chooses to help, can participate in the healing and transformation of the planet and themselves.